TAMING THE TIGER

TAMING THE TIGER

Tibetan Teachings on Right
Conduct, Mindfulness, and
Universal Compassion

Akong Tulku Rinpoche

Inner Traditions
Rochester, Vermont

Inner Traditions International
One Park Street
Rochester, Vermont 05767
www.gotoit.com

LIBRARY OF CONGRESS CATALOGING-IN-PUBLICATION DATA
Akong Tulku, Rinpoche
    Taming the tiger : Tibetan teachings on right conduct, mindfulness, and universal compassion / Akong Tulku Rinpoche.
        p. cm.
    ISBN 0-89281-569-8
    1. Religious life—Buddhism. 2. Buddhism—Doctrines. I. Title.
BQ7775.A56   1995
294.3'444—dc20   95-31532
                                                                                    CIP

Printed and bound in the United States

10 9 8 7 6 5 4 3 2

Distributed to the book trade in Canada by Publishers Group West (PGW), Toronto, Ontario

*This book is dedicated
to the growth of humility, peace and understanding
in the world.*

Illustrations

We are very grateful to The Twelfth Khentin Tai Situpa for kindly doing the calligraphies and drawings for the first part of this book.

Contents

Introduction

There is an almost endless number of books available nowadays that have been written by deeply spiritual people or edited from their lectures and teachings. With there already being so many precious jewels of wisdom, I do not really feel there to be a need for adding my own limited contribution. However, quite a few people have requested the publication of some of the advice I have tried to give in various centres over the last fifteen years, feeling that it might help my students and those whom I have been unable to meet at Kagyü Samyé Ling or the various Samyé Dzongs associated with me.

In response to their sincere requests, and in the hope that somewhere a little benefit may emerge, I have agreed to the publication of this book in which I have tried to share the limited knowledge I possess. I am a very immature person myself, without too much understanding, and know that the advice I can give will only be able to help those either as simple-minded as myself or those even worse off. I apologise to anyone reading these words who is very learned or spiritually pure, for surely they will find them lacking. However, if you are a beginner like me, then the benefit you will derive from these words, as you read and study, will probably depend a great deal upon the amount of effort you put into your learning and upon the degree of your motivation really to progress. I am sure that some of you will find a little help – some more, some less.

The real benefit is in the development of peace and mutual understanding – understanding of the world and of the people around us and of ourselves too. When there is that, then one's wisdom is useful both for oneself and others. Its value will radiate out to one's family, one's society and even to whole nations.

The first section is based upon general advice for everyday life. It looks at the way in which we experience situations and difficulties. The second section gives ways of coping with these difficulties by the use of different mental exercises. How these latter should be classified I am not sure. They may be thought of, and used, as meditations, relaxation techniques for the body and mind, or as mental therapy. In themselves they carry no particular label. I am neither special nor learned and I do not have the power to solve everyone's problems. Far from that, I am just like anyone else. I simply offer you these techniques as a friend.

We are often looking for a different world, a heaven somewhere on earth. But whether this, our life, becomes heaven or hell is something which finally depends entirely upon ourselves; upon what we are inside and upon our motives. It seems to me that the greatest need is for us to work simply and slowly, step by step, and for there to be a gradual progress towards better understanding. Then I think that heaven will appear in our lives and we will not need to yearn for it as a Shangri-la somewhere outside.

I hope that this book may help bring closer understanding between people and between nations. To that end I dedicate any wholesomeness and virtue it may produce.

Dr. Akong Tulku Rinpoche,
Kagyü Samyé Ling, April 1994.

Editor's Preface

Those who have met Akong Rinpoche will be aware of his humility and know his humanity, his readiness to help, and also the very down-to-earth, compassionate nature of his teachings. His guiding instructions on the practice of Dharma, the teachings of Lord Buddha, apply to a whole range of people, from those with families, jobs and children right through to Buddhist monks and nuns. The clarity and simplicity of the teachings make them useful and available to everyone.

Trying to express the nature of his teachings just through the printed word is very difficult. So much of what he teaches is through his example to others. He always has stability and maintains a sense of space in whatever situation arises. His humour will often take the poison out of a situation when things become too heavy or too much of a 'big deal'. Working with the advice and exercises that were put together to make this book has helped me a great deal. It's very hard to do justice to his powerful and direct style of teaching and this book only hints at the depth and richness of his vast understanding. However, Rinpoche's approach is that we should always do our best and be satisfied with that.

Taming the Tiger itself is edited from notes and tapes of Rinpoche's lectures. It also contains original material that he has kindly added in the process of its development. No book is ever completely perfect but the best has been done to communicate Rinpoche's guidance and instructions as faithfully and accurately as possible.

In the thirty years that Rinpoche has been living in the West, he has given teachings in Europe, America and South Africa. He has seen the kind of difficulties that Westerners face. The pressures, tensions and speed of modern living are not the best environment for relaxation or meditation. So the teachings in this book are given by Rinpoche out of the compassionate wish to help people in their everyday lives. The exercises will develop awareness and create a space whereby we can see our world more clearly and be relaxed and open to everything within and around us.This way we can go beyond the ego which is always trying to make its dreams into reality. Instead we can come to understand that our everyday reality is like a dream and not suffer so much.

Taming the Tiger arose from repeated requests, particularly from the ever-growing number of Rinpoche's students who rarely have the opportunity to see him face to face, in order that he could make his teachings available to everyone who needs them. For his students, it is to refresh our memories and remind us of his advice. For others, it is an introduction to the reasons for training the mind and how to go about it. May it serve as an inspiration for everyone.

Clive Holmes

Acknowledgements

We wish to express our gratitude to all who have contributed to the making of this book.

To Rob Nairn of Kagyü Samyé Ling, whose original transcription of a therapy course taught by Akong Rinpoche in South Africa in 1983 served as a basis for the development of Part II.

To Colin Betts for re-writing the initial draft of this book.

To Vin Harris and Phil Johnson who contributed notes and insight to the development of the text.

To Bill Watson for editorial assistance, Hanna Hündorf and Wendy Swan for help with general editing.

To Hanna Hündorf and Ashley Mago-Tovar for helping with the production of this book.

To Hylda Bruyes for unstinting contribution to the courses in Edinburgh which were the main proving ground for the exercises.

To students of courses in many places in Britain, Europe, America and South Africa whose questions and responses to the contents of the book have helped to mould it into its present shape.

Clive Holmes
Edie Irwin

Taming the Tiger

A controlled mind is conducive to happiness
Gautama Buddha

The mind is the root of all our experience, both of ourselves and of others. If we perceive the world in an unclear way, confusion and suffering will surely arise. It is like someone with defective vision seeing the world as being upside down, or a fearful person finding everything frightening. We may be largely unaware of our ignorance and wrong views, yet at present the mind can be compared to a wild tiger, rampaging through our daily lives. Motivated by desire, hatred and bewilderment this untamed mind blindly pursues what it wants and lashes out at all that stands in its way, with little or no understanding of the way things really are.

The wildness we have to deal with is not simply that of anger and rage; it is much more fundamental than that. The tendency to be driven by ignorance, hatred and delusion enslaves us, allowing confusion and negative emotions to predominate. Thus the mind becomes wild and uncontrollable and our freedom is effectively destroyed.

Normally we are so blind that we are unaware of how wild our minds really are. When things go wrong we tend to blame other people and circumstances, rather than look inside ourselves for the causes of the suffering. But if we are ever to find true peace or happiness it is that wildness within which must be faced and dealt with. Only then can we learn to use our energy in a more positive and balanced way, so that we stop causing harm to ourselves and to others.

Before we can tame the tiger we must first track it down. Neither goal is at all easy to achieve, but the difficulties and dangers simply have to be faced. If a child is weak and underdeveloped it isn't helpful just to let that child have its own way. It is the parents' responsibility to encourage the child to walk, so that its body may grow properly and become strong. Thus firmness on the part of the parents can be seen to be a manifestation of true compassion. Similarly, although training the mind might be difficult, even painful at first, we still have to go ahead and do it.

The teachings in *Taming the Tiger* are applicable to anyone who is suffering, not only to oriental people or to Buddhists. Eastern people may differ from Westerners in their facial features, manner of dress, customs and ways of talking, but human nature is universal and runs deeper than mere racial characteristics or skin-colouring. Kindness, wherever it is shown, generally evokes a favourable response; while its opposite causes anger, sorrow or pain. When we consider the joy and suffering in a direct and practical way, it becomes clear that the mind, which is behind everything we do or say, is essentially the same, East or West. Yet where is this mind? We have only to look at everyday situations and examine our behaviour, our desires and our suffering in our everyday situations in order to detect its presence.

As human beings there is a great deal of desire and attachment in our lives. This can cause much suffering, both to ourselves and to others. If the desire is unfulfilled we become unhappy. Even when we get what we want the happiness is only temporary, because invariably a new desire arises to take its place. Time after time all we are doing is trying to satisfy desires which are limitless, shapeless and as vast as the sky.

The process is repeated throughout our lives. As children we want lots of toys – one is not enough – and we soon tire of each, in turn. Later on we may have educational ambitions, or wish to have lots of friends. Desire makes us strive to collect material possessions; own a whole range of different clothes; to buy special kinds of food; to collect property, cars, radios and televisions. Less obviously, we may wish to be beautiful or to avoid sickness for as long as we live. We might even fall ill in order to attract attention, sympathy, kindness. Yet as soon as we succeed in becoming ill we want to be well again.

Similarly, our attitude to eating may be affected: when our stomachs are full, we want them to be empty; when empty, we wish they were full. In all these many ways we constantly search for and dream about what we haven't got, without ever finding true satisfaction. Despite all our effort, hardship and expense, we constantly fail to fulfil our wishes.

The mistake is that we expect to find happiness outside ourselves, failing to realise that it can only come from within. If we admire a particular flower and pick it, within days its beauty has gone. But as it withers and dies the desire remains and we want another flower. Clearly our desire cannot be eternally satisfied by any one flower; rather it requires an endless supply of them. So what is required is a change in the way that we perceive the world. We have to learn to accept our desire and yet not be driven by it, only then will we be content with what we already have instead of constantly wanting more.

Desire is limitless. It is said that since the mind has no form and no finite end then likewise desire has no form, no finite end – it is shapeless, it just goes on and on. Only by taming the mind, therefore, can the endless search for gratification be pacified and our understanding be developed. At that stage we become a little more mature, a little more grown up.

Of course, to some extent, our minds are trained already. When we are babies, we simply act, move and make noises on impulse. Later on as we grow older we do learn some control and independence. Enduring hardships and relating with others grants us a measure of understanding, and some maturity does develop naturally. So, it could be said that we have tamed the tiger a little, in living and growing from day to day. Yet this is still not riding the tiger.

Gurdjieff expresses mind-training in terms of a wild horse and its trainer. Wild horses are neither trained by being completely left alone, nor by continual beating. Such extreme measures will inevitably fail. We have to find a middle way. On the one hand, no benefit comes from the negative attitude that it isn't worthwhile to try and train the wild horse at all. On the other hand, we have to accept that the horse is wild and have a compassionate approach towards training it. Perhaps most important of all, the horse must also accept us as its trainer.

Maturity is only possible once we accept who we are. It isn't helpful to justify our own wildness by blaming society, our family, or our enemies. We have to reach some kind of agreement with ourselves as we really are and accept our thinking, whether it be good or bad. So whatever thoughts which may arise are allowed to flow through us, without our acting them out impulsively, or trying to suppress them, to make them our prisoners.

For example, if we separate out the bad thoughts and instead of accepting them try to hide them in a rubbish bag, then at some stage the bag will become so full that it will burst. This could lead to mental illness and, just like an untamed tiger, we could do a lot of damage, cause a lot of harm. Instead we can work with and transform what is negative; the power of the tiger can be put to good use.

The correct approach is to train the tiger in a dignified way, in a very accepting way. We accept the tiger even if we can't directly see it. The important thing is to face the situation as it is. Irrespective of whether or not we are religious, men or women, young or old, all our sufferings are quite similar; only the causes of those sufferings differ substantially. If we are elderly, for example, we experience the suffering that accompanies old age; if middle-aged, the suffering of jobs and relationships; and if we are young, we have the suffering of education, of growing up. Throughout our lives we are faced with a continual series of sufferings, according to the development and changes of our bodies.

Although the varieties of suffering may be many, and its intensity and degree may change, there is only one effective way of freeing ourselves from the pain of our existence, and that is to accept it. We still deal with our daily life situations but we stop trying to make the whole world conform to our desires and projections. If we are old, we come to accept being old; if we are young, we accept that too whatever the situation, we simply accept it. Once this acceptance occurs, then to a large extent we are freed from the suffering. Once we are able to let it go, it just falls away from us.

This is not to imply that the solution is to develop total inactivity and passivity in relation to the world. Nor should we maintain an endless struggle to make our lives perfect. Instead we follow a middle way, between the two extremes. Having accepted the limitations of being human, we are content to do our best in any situation and to behave in a flexible way according to the level of our understanding, aware both of our own development and the situation as we find it. Our aim throughout is to be completely free from the causes of suffering and to stop creating new suffering for ourselves and others.

First of all we seek to remedy our own suffering. The way of accomplishing this is very much the same wherever one is. Once we accept that the causes of suffering lie mainly in the mind's inability to fulfil its desires, we can see that these causes are internal and are not simply products of our external environment. Whatever society we come from, whether we are spiritual people or not, the understanding that desire arises within our own mind allows us to begin to go forward. We will become aware that others suffer just as we do, and compassion will arise spontaneously. Further, it becomes clear that they, just like us, want only to be happy.

Compassion means the wish to benefit all beings and free them from the causes of suffering. However, when we 'blame' ourselves for the difficulties arising in our own minds it may appear that we lack compassion towards ourselves. And if we have no compassion for ourselves, how then can we cultivate it towards others? In fact it isn't a question of 'blame' at all, nor are we trying to torture or punish ourselves. We are simply acknowledging that desire arises inside our own minds and nowhere else. Such acceptance awakens confidence and wisdom within us and we begin to realise that desire arises in the minds of others just as it does in our own. At that point we are able to coordinate ourselves with others and compassion for them grows. Then there will come a time of true friendship.

Understanding how to tame the mind is beneficial for everyone, not just for beginners. We may think that we know a great deal and have a wide knowledge of life, but for all of us the important thing, the essential and first thing is to tame the mind. This way we can develop compassion and feel friendship for ourselves and others, rather than enmity. There is a Tibetan saying that it's very easy to make enemies, but to develop friendship takes a long, long time. The way beyond suffering lies in the development of friendship within our families, our society and between nations everywhere. We try to be kind to one another, always.

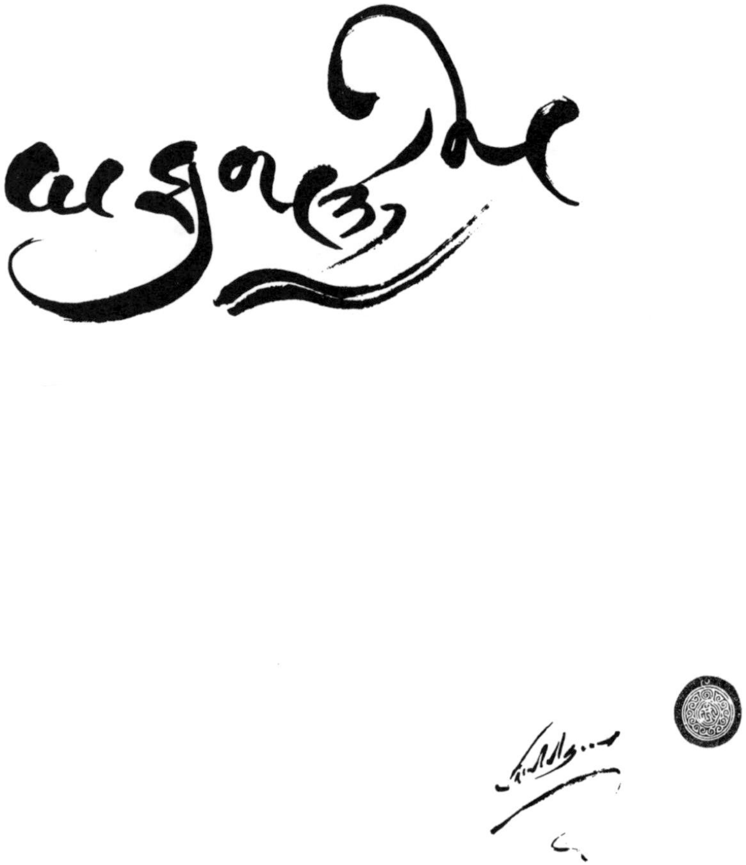

Precious Human Birth

Rare as a daytime star is this precious human birth
Gampopa's Jewel Ornament of Liberation

It is very important to understand right now just how useful this particular body is and how precious is our time. There's no need to wait for misfortune to occur before our minds turn in this direction. If we had full appreciation of how fortunate we are, we would try to develop our minds now, while we have the chance.

In a worldly way, we already consider our lives to be precious and strive to preserve our own existence. The trouble is that we generally identify ourselves by, and with, its least valuable aspects. The ordinary sense of 'preciousness' consists of trying to protect the body from getting old, sick, cold, or hungry, rarely considering that one day it is bound to die. On the whole we'd like to be rich, healthy and beautiful forever. When we don't like something we try to change it; whilst if unwelcome developments occur we'll do anything rather than face up to them. As humans we are caught up in a continual cycle of happiness and suffering. We may easily miss the point of our existence in our preoccupation with relationships, possessions, appearance, work and entertainment.

Essentially, however, we are capable of very much more. Even unintelligent beings like insects and animals want to preserve their bodies in a warm, comfortable way and avoid suffering. If we limit ourselves to these pre-occupations, without seeing beyond them, we are failing to make the most of our far greater opportunities – our potential is being wasted.

So we need to realise just how much we are capable of achieving, both for our own good and for others. This understanding will enable us to progress towards living in a useful and worthwhile way. Even one person can bring great benefit to the world. The Buddha, for example, has helped billions of people through his teaching. So also have Jesus Christ and the Prophet Mohammed. Similarly the work of such great scientists as Edison and Pasteur has been of enormous value to mankind. Although we may not achieve so much, or become rich and famous, with determination and diligent effort we too can fulfil our potential. We will already have achieved a great deal if we can bring happiness and freedom from suffering to ourselves and to those around us.

At times it may seem that taming the mind is unnecessary, that we are happy enough already, but such happiness easily can be lost; it is useless to pretend otherwise. Like the sand-castles that children build beside the sea, sooner or later the tide comes in and washes them away. Material pleasures and happiness are temporary at best, and often are of benefit only to oneself.

On the other hand, the happiness arising from deep inner development has stability, it increases all the time and is useful to others. It's like a magic fire that continues to burn brightly even when cold water is poured onto it. For example if someone is angry with us, normally we would react negatively. However, if we are able to be patient and appreciate the pain that the other person is feeling, then compassion follows naturally and we will increase our understanding. If there were no negative circumstances, how could we tame our minds and cultivate limitless compassion, limitless joy? So it can be seen that worldly happiness and the happiness of a patient and mature mind are really quite different.

The right way to live is to learn to put into practice the aim to benefit everyone. When we merely look after ourselves, the benefit is limited to one person only. But if we have the intention to help all beings, then our lives can become more and more valuable. The more we are able to do this, the more valuable our lives will become. As with a car battery, the more the car is used, the greater the charge in the battery; but if the car stands idle, the battery becomes flat and useless. Thus when our lives are used fruit-fully, strength is gained rather than lost. If, on the other hand, we fail to appreciate the value of our lives, we may waste both time and precious opportunity – and time and opportunity wasted are gone forever.

Helping others does not mean we should neglect ourselves. We still have to treat our bodies with respect and take care of our health and appearance; for to cause distress or harm to anyone, including ourselves, would be unkind and is not the way. But once we are able to look after ourselves then we can go on to help others. At that time our strength and capability may be put to good use for the benefit of all beings without distinction. This universal compassion and loving-kindness will bring value and purpose to our lives, leading to the full development of our potential.

The aim is not to be too involved in our own concerns. We continue to enjoy life but in a different way from before – mindful that when we indulge or harm ourselves we cheapen something precious, and effectively cheat all other beings. Reliance on drugs, smoking, or drinking too much alcohol, for example, brings no benefit to anyone in the long term. The effects of everything that causes suffering, even if not obvious at the time, will definitely manifest later.

In order to understand correctly the value of the precious human birth it is necessary to think deeply about it. One difficulty is that we tend to underestimate its rarity. However, we have only to look around us to appreciate our good fortune. The countless animals, birds, insects and fish are all at the mercy of their environment, with no chance at all of going beyond the suffering they experience (in their current existence). Even amongst humans there are very few with the understanding or inclination to follow a spiritual path. In Tibet there's a saying that to have a precious human birth is as rare as a daytime star. Thinking like this will help us to appreciate our lives, the rare opportunity they offer, and to count our considerable blessings.

At the moment we may consider that our lives lack purpose and worth. Yet, despite our problems and sufferings, the potential does exist for us to make a valuable and worthwhile contribution to the world we live in. We all have something to give, it's just a question of learning what and how. One pound well spent can do a great deal of good whereas one million pounds used unwisely could cause only suffering. No matter how much we have, when we use it for the best reasons and in a skilful way, the result will be beneficial. So the richness we have to offer is not dependent on external factors like personal power, possessions or the approval of other people. Clearly to attach too much value to our physical experience or living conditions can create unhappiness.

However, for those with right understanding, it doesn't matter whether they live in a tower block, a prison, a monastery or a palace. Having achieved genuine and lasting peace and equanimity within their minds, they are happy wherever they find themselves. If we can follow their example, and learn how to plant and cultivate the enlightened motivation of compassion, we will be taking advantage of the rare opportunity given by our precious human birth.

Impermanence

Like stars, mists and candleflames,
Mirages, dew-drops and water-bubbles
Like dreams, lightning and clouds.
In that way I will view all composite phenomena.
Kagyü Wishing Prayer

Even with awareness of the potential within us, if we fail to understand the impermanence of everything, we will delay our development. In order to relate correctly to impermanence, we must understand its true nature. Then we can apply this knowledge to our experience.

First we examine the outer environment, all that we perceive through our senses. The four seasons, for example, are characterised by changing climatic conditions, degrees of warmth and coldness, light and darkness. We might prefer the summertime, but we still have to accept winter when it comes, for to wish the one to stay forever and the other not to arrive is the kind of desire that never can be fulfilled. Instead, we try to appreciate the seasonal changes; the variety of different birds and flowers, the leaves turning green to gold, then gone; the earth going from brown to white and back again. Everywhere, in everything we can see the essence of impermanence. We look at it and can see that it is really something very beautiful.

Changes occur in the particulars of our own lives, too. From being poor we become rich; from rich, poor. One day we lose a

job, another day we find one; or one day we are the boss, the next
a servant. In the world of politics these uncertainties are especially
acute. Many leaders hold great power for a few years at most
before being voted out, overthrown or even shot. While the
changes affecting our own careers may not be quite so dramatic,
they happen all the same.

Neither do our inner lives and feelings escape the workings of
impermanence. From the moment we wake up until we go to sleep
at night, nothing stays the same for very long. Our moods rise and
fall, our hopes and fears come and go all the time. Often we are
greatly affected by outside influences. We might meet a good
friend for the first time in years and get very excited. Moments
later the arrival of an enemy at once turns our feelings upside-
down. If we can imagine a monkey jumping up and down at the
windows of an empty house, we will have some idea of what kind
of mind we have. Like the monkey, our emotions are up one
minute, down the next.

Nothing whatever is permanent. We were born, grew up,
went to school, grew older, and sooner or later we will die. Our
lives get shorter every moment and there is nothing we can do
about it. When death comes all of our friends and family, property
and possessions will have to be left behind. We could become
rather frightened or depressed about this, but that would not be
accepting impermanence in a positive way. Instead we should
acknowledge that such a change is at some stage inevitable and
resolve to live the rest of our lives in a more worthwhile and compassionate way. Moreover, realising that others share the same
fate can inspire us to greater kindness toward the people with
whom we live and work right now.

At the moment we tend to use our spare time looking for
enjoyment and the fulfilment of our desires. We either completely
ignore the training of our minds or leave it until last. Of course, we
all need to relax sometimes; there is no point in going to extremes.
However, a sound understanding of impermanence will inspire us
to spend our time in a more worthwhile way, beneficial in the
longer term rather than just for today and tomorrow.

The true meaning of impermanence is often misunderstood.
We might believe, for example, that owing to impermanence our
jobs or careers are worthless and that we should abandon them.

But this would be a false interpretation, using the truth as an excuse for idleness, a way of escaping the situation. Similarly, if we have some laundry to do and think, "I'm not going to do this because I might die tomorrow," we may well be developing laziness but certainly not our understanding.

These days many younger people find education tiresome and boring, so when they come across the teaching on impermanence they feel it justifies their not studying any more, even though to give it up could upset their parents and friends and cause them suffering. Impermanence does not mean that we should not work or study, it simply states that everything changes.

There is no need to panic or to over-react as soon as we hear about impermanence. Instead we try to use it positively to help us live useful lives. We can watch how everything changes without losing any of our enjoyment or appreciation of life.

Just as there cannot be happiness all the time, so there will not always be sadness. The one turns into the other, quite naturally. But every moment can be accepted as it comes, whatever its emotional colour; and even when there is great suffering, at least we are feeling something and can try to relate to the quality of the experience.

We have to stop imagining that everything exists in a very solid way, either inside or outside ourselves. When we mentally strive to make things more and more fixed, we will suffer when, inevitably, changes occur. Too much involvement with our aversions and desires makes us tend to reject or cling on to the things we experience. Thus we refuse to accept change when it comes and resist it instead. Fighting such a series of losing battles causes our emotions to go up and down all the time, at the expense of our inner stability. The whole point is to realise that everything changes and so develop less attachment to what we are doing.

With our minds untamed we might continue to suffer indefinitely, so it is useful to follow a spiritual path now while we have the chance. There is no time to lose. Although we may prefer to think we go on forever, when we consider the matter carefully and honestly, we see the obvious truth that tomorrow might be too late. We are subject to change, just like everything else.

Impermanence, then, pervades all of the outer world and all our inner experience. We can neither prevent it nor avoid it. It happens all the time. What we can do is to acknowledge it. Accepting it in this way will help us to appreciate what we already have whilst lessening our involvement with it. Realising impermanence will enable us not to get sidetracked in useless pursuits. Instead we can mature our minds by simply applying this understanding throughout our lives.

The Right Motivation

May all beings always have happiness and the causes of
happiness
May they all be free from suffering and the causes of suffering
May each one never be separate from the true happiness which
has no suffering
And may they always act with understanding of the great
impartiality,
Free from attachment to close ones and aversion to others.
The Four Limitless Contemplations

This prayer represents the right attitude of the awakened state of mind. Although the language may be strange to us, in fact the meaning is quite simple. We all have the essence of the enlightened attitude in our hearts already. Yet because of ignorance, this essential nature has been obscured and covered up by negativity, misunderstandings and by harmful actions. Between our present state of mind and the awakened state, therefore, lies a journey. While for some people the way may be longer than for others, the important thing is that there is a path whereby we can come to lead happy and useful lives. So the prayer expresses both the kind of mind we should aim for and the means by which we should try to attain it.

The right motivation is the wish for the happiness and well-being of everyone, so that all may attain peace and freedom from the causes of suffering. It is this very worthwhile aim that will inspire our efforts, both when times are easy and when they are hard. Although the prayer suggests a high level of understanding, it is useful to state the goal from the outset since its truth and value apply to all stages of the path.

Nowadays many people come to meditation with the wrong motivation. They wish to use meditation to further their own ends, without thinking of anyone else. But hoping to achieve clairvoyance, astral travel, special powers and similar attainments only feeds and strengthens the ego, without increasing understanding at all. Rather than pursuing exciting experiences, our task is to learn how to deal with the mind and help others. Even if such experiences were to occur, they are not the goal or the target and should be left alone.

Another misconception is to see the path of compassion and self development as a means or justification for cutting oneself off from society. This is a negative attitude, however, rather than something useful and beneficial to all. There is something essentially wrong with the motivation when our practice of meditation is used to preserve and confirm our own negativity towards society.

If we were completely happy and free from suffering there would be no need for such a path. However, the fact is that we are ignorant, just as others are ignorant, and for all of us the suffering caused by that ignorance is repeated, day after day. Clearly a path is needed, and recognising this need will motivate us to work our way along it, for the benefit both of ourselves and of all others.

Without some kind of motivation or incentive we would be unlikely to make the effort required to achieve our aims. When we are cold and want to be warm, for example, we're inspired to get up and light a fire. If we were warm already then we simply wouldn't bother to do so. Similarly, if we want a good job, we are prepared to undergo considerable training, hardship even, in order to secure it. In all our activities there is first motivation, followed by intention and some kind of effort. The same process is applicable to meditation, too.

If there were no aim or purpose, why should we put up with all the hard work that may be involved? Since our primary aim is the wish to help all beings, we have to direct our effort towards putting that wish into practice. Whenever we do a meditation session, and throughout our daily lives, all the time we strive to preserve the right attitude and be guided by it.

At our current level, as beginners, we may feel daunted by such a high ideal, reasoning, 'What's the use of someone like me trying to develop the mind? I'm so full of hatred and desire, it's pointless trying to change'. Yet this is precisely why a strong effort is needed. If we already see everything as positive, have great openness towards others and do everything we do for their benefit, then we are in a compassionate state already. Such qualities are like the ABC of the spiritual path: if we know how to read then we don't need to be taught the alphabet; but if we lack the right motivation then it has to be awakened within us.

So if the idea and wish to help others is not there already, it must be introduced, even if it's a forced situation to begin with. We cannot develop compassion unless we have this attitude of benefitting everyone. It is like teaching children the alphabet in order that they can read later on. The attitude of benefitting all beings is what the right motivation is all about.

At present, though, we may wish only to be free of our own suffering. Such a feeling is quite natural, and it's possible we might enjoy such freedom for a short time even without meditation. But we are trying to achieve rather more than this. Instead of always thinking in terms of our own desires, comforts and happiness – quite unconcerned about the welfare of others – our aim here is to develop genuine kindness and compassion for everyone.

The way forward is to identify and ripen the positive qualities that exist within ourselves and all others, and to develop them whenever and however we can. How is this to be achieved? In the first place we shouldn't try to run before we can walk, so we must learn to go forward step by step. First, we generate the right attitude towards ourselves, second to our friends and families, then it is extended to include everyone.

Recognising that the path begins with ourselves is important here. We have to learn to stand on our own two feet and no longer be a burden to others. In the first instance we allow them space and stop contributing to their problems. Trying actively to help someone else without first understanding ourselves could do more harm than good. That would be compassion without wisdom. For example, if someone is drowning in a lake and we try to save them without being able to swim, we both could end up drowning. First we ourselves have to learn to swim. Similarly, only after we have tamed our own mind and know how to deal properly with happiness and suffering alike can we really help others.

It's also important to use our common sense. While it is very good to want to help others, we shouldn't go around looking for ways to force our help upon them. But neither do we have to wait until we're 'perfect' before we can be of use. It is a question of balance, of using our energy wisely. Whereas our current unenlightened state shouldn't be used as an excuse for doing nothing at all, we do have to be careful. When we act as mindfully as possible there will be some benefit, even if we can't yet act in a way that is one hundred percent pure. When we are completely purified then everything we do will be beneficial to others; but in the meantime it's good to give some help now. No matter how limited our ability, by helping as best we can, we will be deepening our understanding and forming the right mental attitude that will later develop into the practice of perfect compassion.

First, then, we develop compassion for ourselves and then go on to develop it towards others. We may, of course, feel that we don't need to do this, that we are very loving and kind already. While it's true that there are often deep and close bonds between husband and wife, brother and sister, friend and friend, true lovingkindness is for this degree of love to embrace everyone. The problem in our society is that we fall in love readily with friends and lovers, even with our possessions, but this kind of love is frequently narrow and limited. There's nothing wrong in loving close friends and relatives. Indeed there can be much good in this, and kindness has to start somewhere, but if we limit our love solely to these people, we are simply creating chains for ourselves. Bonds and ties of this sort work both ways; they can bind as well as comfort us.

So, we try not to restrict our compassion to one particular group or category of people at the expense of others. For example, our feelings easily go out to the poor and the hungry, but it may be difficult for us to generate much compassion for those who are wealthy and well-fed. Although the suffering of these people is more often of a mental nature – worries about losing their wealth or possessions, or about the decisions they have to take – it may be no less acute for that. Poor people have different kinds of suffering, that's all – like the simple problem of whether or not they have enough to eat. We have to learn to extend our compassion to all people; rich or poor, black or white, to everyone.

Right development along these lines will make us much happier, more balanced in our lives, and, as all minds influence each other, the generation of broad and expansive compassion will spontaneously benefit all those around us. Accordingly, as our potential ripens and our strength increases, we become less reliant and dependent on others for support and comfort. However, we must guard carefully against becoming big-headed and proud.

There could be a tendency to think that following a spiritual path makes us very special people who are superior to others in some way. Yet our aim is to serve others, not to be served by them. Developing a compassionate mind doesn't mean lying around expecting other people to fulfil our needs, as if we were kings or queens and they our servants. This kind of pride is a great obstacle to the practice. Neither should we look down on others who are suffering, feeling that there's something wrong with them, or inferior about them. Humility is very important, in fact it lies at the heart of true compassion. We should be prepared to give of ourselves and to make sacrifices for the general good.

Genuine progress consists of developing in a gentle, friendly way, each according to his or her capacity. As long as we are doing our best we can be satisfied that our potential isn't being wasted. As human beings we will surely make mistakes, but there's no need to become neurotic about them or to punish ourselves. We can be sorry we got something wrong without allowing that regret to stand in the way of our development. Instead we use it to strengthen our determination, thinking: 'Although one bridge across the river has fallen, another can be built. No use standing here crying about it.'

As soon as we wake up we should make the commitment that whatever we think, do or say may benefit and be useful to others. To forget our compassion is to lose something very precious. Without it, the true path is closed to us. Whereas physical strength and vitality last for a day or a year or a decade or two at best, the right mental attitude banishes tiredness and hopelessness indefinitely, enabling us to go on helping others all the time, throughout our lives. Until one has met someone who manifests this ability, it is difficult to believe; yet it is the potential within all of us.

Right motivation may be likened to a seed, but one that has to be planted again and again. At first when we plant it, it may appear that we are deceiving ourselves and others, that owing to our attachments and aversions we are unable really to help anyone at all. Yet although at this stage our commitment may be only a form of words, it harms no-one. Later on, when the attitude is no longer strange to us, genuine loving-kindness towards others will grow out of it. As we continue to develop the right motivation, it will become an integral part of our lives, inseparable from us. At that time, our right motivation of compassion will be effortless, consistent, and effective – just the way we are.

Facing the Situation

Don't wallow in self-pity!
Atisha's Seven Points of Mind-Training

Between our first encounter with teachings on the pure nature of mind and the attainment of wisdom and compassion lies a long and often difficult journey. Should we decide to actually make the trip, we must be realistic about how to travel. If we want to get from London to Scotland, just thinking about it won't get us there; we have to actually get into a vehicle and go, whether by car, rail or air. In spite of the inherent difficulties, just avoiding the journey will not give us much satisfaction or take us where we want to go. We must choose a starting point, a vehicle and a path; then get on with it.

In our journey from London to Scotland we head for Euston station, the M1 or Heathrow. In the same way, if our goal is to live happy and useful lives for the benefit of all beings, then we start with the ordinary situations of our daily lives. These are the raw materials for the work, and the experience and understanding they provide are available to everyone, whether educated or not. But first we have to overcome the habitual tendency to neglect or evade the problems associated with the external environment and those with whom we share it, as well as the dissatisfaction and suffering we feel within ourselves.

If we are honest with ourselves we will recognise that in a sense we are all beginners with regard to relating skilfully to the problems in our lives. We may be attracted to exciting meditations such as learning how to levitate or fly, but it is more useful first to learn how to keep our feet on the ground. Also, we may feel we are very advanced already and don't need any teachings, even though unconsciously we may be creating the same suffering for ourselves over and over again. 'Taming the Tiger' is essentially about learning how to accept and deal with the ordinary situations of our daily lives. Unless we acknowledge our need for such instruction, it is highly unlikely that any genuine progress will be achieved.

Having recognised that a path is necessary, we have to travel along it. In a dream world – like Shangri-la – we might sit down with a cigar in one hand, a glass of fine wine in the other, a beautiful lover on either side of us and still achieve deep compassion and understanding. In the real world, however, it does not work that way; we have to make some kind of effort. No amount of wishful thinking will prevent us from meeting with considerable suffering if we fail to deal now with the basic situations of this current existence, and thus neglect the taming of our minds.

First we have to tame our minds and build a solid foundation for our further development. This is very important. We should try to bear in mind the precious opportunity of having a human birth; that all things are impermanent; and that good action leads to happiness, whilst bad unskilful activity causes only suffering. Above all, we should never forget the aim of taming the mind – the development of compassion for the benefit of all beings.

From this starting point, this firm foundation, we can develop gradually, stage by stage. Without it, any progress could easily be obstructed; we might stray from the true path. So we set aside our pride and acknowledge the level that we are really on. No matter how intelligent or successful we are in the worldly sense, as long as we are fearful of losing our wealth, loved ones or possessions – let alone our lives – then we are still in suffering and need to tame the mind. For all of us, the only place to start is at the beginning.

If we were to find a rough diamond and knew how to cut it then we could make a beautiful piece of jewellery and wear it to our advantage. Yet if we didn't know now to cut it properly we might smash it and make it worthless. The exercises and meditations given in this book provide the means to transform and mature the mind. If they are used with skill and care, they will result in making the mind as clear and pure as a cut and polished diamond.

It is important that we try to deal with the situations involving ourselves and others in a way that is relaxed and uncomplicated. This may not be particularly exciting; indeed it might be quite boring. However, we are aiming to accept situations as they are, and fundamentally most of them are very ordinary. Every day there is happiness and unhappiness; there are pleasant things happening and unpleasant things happening. Sometimes our experiences are bitter and sweet at the same time. In other situations, our life experiences may be quite indifferent. What matters is that they are our experiences, ones that we ourselves have to face.

Problems don't always arise due to negative causes. We might be very well off for example, but still suffer from fear of losing what we have, or from not knowing what to do with our wealth. Whatever our circumstances, they have to be understood and dealt with. Some have to be accepted, for better or worse; others worked on and improved. Other people can encourage and support us, but if we want to sort out our lives then we have to do it ourselves.

Many of us are quite skilled at avoiding painful situations, and we all have our favourite way of doing this. We change our job or our address, find a new lover, run to the doctor, or surround ourselves with friends. Or we may fantasise a lot, watch T.V., take drugs, overeat or drink too much. Should these activities fail, we may find ourselves unable to sleep or think properly and become so distressed that we make ourselves ill. We may be tempted to end our lives altogether, even though this would be as bad as killing someone else. Feeling sorry for ourselves can lead to all kinds of problems, without providing any solution to them. So we see that there are many different ways in which we can forget our intention to develop compassion both toward ourselves or others.

Avoiding or escaping situations merely takes our mind off our problems without actually doing anything to solve them. If we merely do what we like and don't do what we don't like, our difficulties only increase and will recur again and again. Meanwhile we could be damaging our health as well as our mind, and getting into all sorts of bad habits which become stronger and harder to break. When we give in to weakness, we just get weaker and less likely to rid ourselves of suffering in the longer term. A farmer may use tons of fertiliser to get a good harvest for a few years only to find later that he has exhausted and poisoned the soil. So we should use a little wisdom here; not thinking so much of short-term remedies, but instead seeking solutions that will bring lasting benefit and help us go beyond the causes of suffering.

This does not mean we should relate to the situations we find disagreeable in a rigid, inflexible way. Taking things too seriously can be as harmful as living in a completely frivolous way. In the first case we may lose our sense of humour and tend to view life as a struggle; whilst in the second, we risk living entirely in a fantasy world. Either way, we lose touch with our everyday lives and consequently with our true feelings in relation to them. This also happens when we are overwhelmed by negative emotions such as anger or jealousy, or when we are obsessed with the past or the future. We must guard against losing sight of the world as it is right now, the world we actually live in.

So far we have concentrated on what happens when we try to run away from our problems. By training the mind, however, we can learn to confront and deal effectively with what we currently perceive to be painful or distressing. For example, the very act of facing up to situations frees us from the struggle to escape from them! At this point we might well be surprised to find that what is troubling us is really not so big, bad or important as we had imagined.

Once we are ready to accept the way things are, even the apparently hellish aspects of life can be transformed. All we need are the means and the will to accomplish this transformation. If, on the other hand, we give in to faint-heartedness or put things off, the bad will probably get worse. So we must acknowledge our experiences and commitments for what they are, whether difficult, easy or just plain ordinary. The important thing is not to become strongly affected emotionally by our perception of these circumstances and by the value-judgements we associate with them.

Unfortunately, our background as members of a modern civilised country does little to equip us for accepting things as they are. Our kind of society has an altogether different approach to situations which are held to be disagreeable or imperfect in some way. For example, we invent complicated machinery in order to take the boredom out of certain kinds of work. Then we have to make lots of people redundant, leaving them more bored than they were before. Moreover, we bulldoze whole communities and build high-rise flats to improve living-standards, only to find that no-one wants to live in them; while the people who must live in them, feel isolated and miserable. We are always trying to increase and improve things without realising the consequences, or knowing where to stop.

Rather than directing all our energy into futile attempts to make life perfect, we could be using some of this effort to develop our tolerance and appreciation of the way things are. Such inner peace brings deep and lasting happiness; whilst the joy derived from worldly pursuits, objects and other people is invariably impermanent. We have a clear choice to make between allowing ourselves to be blown about like a feather, this way and that on the wind of change, acting and reacting to whatever comes along; or to work towards establishing some kind of stability within ourselves, independent of chance and fortune, praise or blame.

If we choose correctly, then real understanding and equanimity will take root and grow steadily within us. In time we will be able to transform all of our experience and relate to its positive qualities, rather than be affected by what we perceive to be its negative ones. At this stage we can be grateful to other people who are rude, unkind or dishonest with us because we have learned to use their ill-will to develop our patience and compassion. The idea is not to go around looking for trouble, but if problems and difficulties should arise, we can live with them and use them to advantage, without giving in to unhappiness and despair.

Developing such an attitude is, of course, much easier said than done. In fact, we have to put in a lot of hard work. The problem is that in the Western tradition we are conditioned to believe that strength and happiness come from outside ourselves so that we do not look for them within. We have to be prepared to try a new approach. At this stage what is needed is a mirror, so that we can see how we are right now. Then we can clean and transform what is already there and awaken the confidence and strength within us.

The Mirror

Samsara is the tendency to find fault with others
Naropa

We have heard that when we look for happiness outside of ourselves, we are looking in the wrong place. We could introduce any amount of variety to our experience, even travel to lots of different places, but we would still see everything through the same eyes. It is how we think and feel that colours our perception of the world we live in.

When we try to change the world and make it conform to our expectations and preferences we are bound to fail. If it's raining, we can't make it sunny just by wishing it so; but we can deal with the part of ourselves which is bothered by the rain. This doesn't mean that we need a new personality – we have a personality already. In practical terms what is needed is a mirror to show us precisely who we are and which aspects of ourselves would benefit from being worked on.

Up to now we've tended to build up a collection of masks, different masks for different situations, but we've never really examined our true face because in a sense we're too close to the subject to see it clearly. Instead we look at other people, and when we see a beautiful face we hope that is the way we look too.

Sometimes, however, our mask slips, or we forget to put it on, and then we glimpse the way we really are. Usually this is so painful that we just can't take it. We have to cover up again as quickly as possible. We're so used to trying to change things that we can't even accept ourselves as we are. Meanwhile, under the mask, our true face is turning rotten for want of air and light, and because we never thought of cleaning it properly.

On the surface we may appear to be a good person, but it's the one underneath the mask that needs to be purified. If our minds are pure, then we really will be useful to others. However, pretending to be good, whilst remaining rotten inside, will not be much use either to ourselves or anyone else.

Behind the mask is the self we have to learn to understand and work with. All of us wear the label 'I' but we don't really know who we are. When we give away something as small as a crust of bread, we think we're being so good and helpful and we go on remembering that act of kindness for a long time. On the other hand, when we do something selfish or bad, we try to forget it at once. We tend to build a false image of ourselves in order to comfort ourselves. This form of self-deception is very difficult to penetrate – that's why we need the mirror.

In Tibet there was a great and famous teacher called Lodro Thaye Jamgon Kongtrul Rinpoche who once expressed the problem as follows: 'When I look at "spiritual" practitioners I see that on the outside they may dress very smartly and talk nicely but when I look inside their minds they are just like snakes, filled with poison. Whenever they meet obstacles, or when difficulties arise, then their true mind may be seen. Just as a snake will bite even though it looks quite smooth, so these people will strike out if anyone threatens them in any way.'

It isn't, of course, that the snake itself is bad; it has the potential to be either good or bad, but through fear, hatred and ignorance it becomes able to kill whenever it feels itself threatened. Similarly, whatever we see inside ourselves as bad arises from ignorance, which can and must be transformed into wisdom. When we begin to turn our mind inward and purify what we find there, the way will have been found, and all external situations will automatically become easier to deal with in a useful, positive way.

It is important, though, to have a balanced attitude towards what we see in the mirror. To see only the bad side is as harmful and fruitless as to see only the good one. Dwelling on the negative aspects of the personality could lead to deep depression and hopelessness. We can examine ourselves in the mirror without condemning what we see there or wishing to smash the entire picture. On the other hand, to ignore or suppress our negative side will only strengthen it, leading to a build-up of inner pressure that one day is likely to explode.

These days many of us get angry about nuclear weapons, yet in a sense there is a kind of nuclear reaction going on inside our minds all the time. Every day the ego generates pride, jealousy, anger, desire and hatred which spread fear and tension in all directions, causing harm to ourselves and others. To neutralise a nuclear weapon or reaction it's no use simply to bury it and wish it away. Similarly, to make harmless the destructive forces within ourselves we have to defuse and dismantle them with great care and skill, by means of our compassion and understanding. This difficult task has to be approached with patience and calm detachment.

What we learn from looking into 'the mirror' can be very useful on the path, but first it has to become part of our general experience and not remain separate from it. For if we don't integrate the understanding and compassion that is awakened, we are merely putting on another mask.

If we are ordinary men and women and want to learn to defend ourselves, then there is far more benefit in learning to do so as men and women rather than imagining we are elephants and learning self-defence as elephants. There is no harm in pretending to be an elephant, but if there is no relationship to what is actually happening, then it is a waste of time. What is being considered or visualised must be applied in our ordinary lives. To spend an hour meditating on removing jealousy, for example, and then, once the session is over, to be immediately drawn into a jealous confrontation is not very helpful at all. What is being considered has to be applied to our daily lives, to the ordinary situations which make up our existence.

Moreover, we could study and collect lots of different teachings with the best motivation in the world, but unless they can be related and applied to our particular circumstances there won't be much benefit. Formal education and intellectual ability are of some help in understanding and dealing with the situations of daily life; but an open, accepting mind is more important.

Although within us all there is this great potential for understanding and compassion, unless we develop these qualities and put them to good use they might as well not exist. A wealthy man who does not know how to use his money suffers more than a poor man who spends each penny in a useful way. Someone might have one car and a hundred batteries but if he allows the batteries to go flat, his car still won't start.

So we have to be mindful and make the best use of what we have. It isn't enough simply to be aware, for example, of a jealous feeling inside. If we are to tame and transform it, we have to apply a certain amount of skill and effort. In this way our confidence and strength can increase, feelings of poverty and helplessness will give way to a sense of richness and self-respect. As we continue to use the mirror some improvement will become evident in what we see there, confirming that spiritual progress is taking place; and the pain we felt before will lessen and gradually disappear.

One by one, stage by stage, we will be able to identify and neutralise the inner poisons and negative states of mind which are making the world so difficult to live in. None of us can completely master the outside world, but we can defeat the anger, pride, desire, hatred and jealousy within that set us at odds with it. At that stage all sense of being in conflict with external situations will cease. We can make friends with ourselves as well as with the world, and we'll be able to help all those with whom we share it. Everything and everyone will be useful to us, and we to them.

In the meantime we should guard against becoming obsessed with ourselves and our problems. If we remember the right motivation we'll be more likely to keep a sense of perspective and proportion. The aim is to use what we see for the benefit of everyone, which implies an expansive attitude of mind, an objective point of view. Thus we are able to see things clearly, as they are, and can correctly assess what is unbalanced in our lives – changing what can be changed, but also accepting what has to be accepted.

To live with a mirror in front of us isn't easy, but in order to understand and sort out our problems it's worth putting up with a certain amount of distress and discomfort. Force of habit means we are more used to judging and trying to change others, so having to face up to and work on ourselves could be rather frightening. It's quite normal to fear the unknown; the solution is to get to know and to make friends with ourselves, just as the successful trainer first wins the tiger's confidence. Having achieved a workable relationship with ourselves, we may find that we do not have as many problems as we thought we had, and those that do exist dissolve more easily.

This way of working with ourselves is not only appealing, it is also one that must be genuinely and sincerely taken to heart. So let us sort out our own problems. We must tame our minds and train ourselves. The alternative is to remain indefinitely in some degree of conflict with the world at large, blaming other people and external situations for whatever disturbs or upsets us. There are several billions of people we will have to sort out if we approach the problem in that way. Rather than trying to change them all let us 'look in the mirror', work on ourselves the way we are and take on the slightly less difficult task of taming and training our own minds.

Body, Speech and Mind

If you can help others it is very good,
Yet if you cannot do this,
At least do not harm them.
His Holiness the Dalai Lama

Whenever difficulties arise, or when there is suffering in our lives, we tend to blame other people or circumstances outside of our control. Rather than appreciating the inherent purity of others, we often find it easier to project our own negativity on to a convenient outer form. Thus, we think that the way that others act, talk or think is the cause of any anger, jealousy or other negative emotion which we may feel. This is a mistaken view of the world and of ourselves. Instead we should come to terms with and try to sort out our own problems and shortcomings. Then we may find that there are no longer so many difficulties, and that those which remain are not beyond our control. In practical terms, it is clearly easier to wear sandals than to attempt to cover the entire road with leather.

We stop pretending that our problems are someone else's fault and we stop concealing our own faults behind various masks. It is wrong to think that smart clothes can make our bodies perfect; that silence will perfect our speech in some way; and that because no one can see our mind it doesn't matter if we think bad thoughts. The way forward is to drop these masks, see ourselves as we really are and face up to this. The everyday situations of our lives, whether they are boring or dramatic, show us in our true light. These are the situations we have to deal with – they are our business.

In order to isolate and identify the causes of suffering, first we have to try to understand how we experience our world. It is useful to consider this in terms of body, speech and mind.

Whether young, middle-aged, or elderly, each of us has a body consisting of flesh, blood, bones and other matter, which experiences a variety of feelings and sensations. Similarly, we have the ability to speak and communicate although what we say may or may not be true. Finally, we have the creator of good and bad thoughts and feelings which we call mind. At the moment, as far as we are concerned, this body, speech and mind have a real and solid existence.

What we do is expressed in movement and physical activity and what we say finds expression through speech and sound; but all that is good or bad inside us has its origin in the mind. In this respect body and speech respond like a muppet being operated by the mind. The trouble is that we've been so busy trying to organize people and external situations that our own wires have grown rusty from lack of use – they need a little oil. At the moment, then, something isn't quite right. The muppet is failing to perform or behave in a way which we can feel happy about, and this clumsiness and inefficiency are giving rise to any number of problems and disappointments.

Ideally, the body would faithfully serve the mind in a harmony which implies no separation. If, instead, we allow the body to follow its own base inclinations, we could easily become ensnared in a sensual, materialistic existence from which escape would be very difficult. This trap awaits both the careless and wilful alike, but has the same result in either case – loss of freedom. So, we need to learn how to pull the strings more skilfully, better to translate what we genuinely mean and believe into what we say or do.

This is not to say that we should deny the needs of our bodies or suppress the natural wisdom that speaks through them. Our guiding principle should be compassion. In this sense compassion may be defined as the conviction that since we ourselves are richly-endowed and potentially enlightened beings, we have a lot to offer the world and its inhabitants. We plant this seed, this positive attitude, in our minds and allow it to pervade and inform all that we say and do. This unifies our body, speech and mind in a common purpose, so that each acts in harmony with the other at all times, at every level of consciousness and in all modes of expression. Compassion is the seed and the beginning, also the path and the goal.

If we hold out our hand to a dog, it may approach us, expecting food or friendship; but if we raise our hand to it, that same dog will run away, suspecting that we mean it harm. In the same way, every move, sound or thought we create has some effect on others. We have only to look around to confirm that this is so. For example, the way we move sends signals to other people, whether intentionally or not. If someone limps we assume they have rheumatism, or have been in an accident at some time. If we see someone swinging his or her hips when they walk past, we might find it sexy and imagine that the message is aimed at us, even though that person may be quite unaware of the signal we are receiving. Body language is a powerful means of communication. So if we want our bodies to make their presence felt in a helpful and positive way, we have to learn to act mindfully, aware that our gestures affect all those around us, as well as provoking reactions that may bounce back on us.

Similarly we have to be mindful of the sounds we make, the things we say. Sounds and words which are kind and gentle will have a good effect on the minds of others, encouraging them and providing comfort. Even someone in deep suffering may be freed from it just by hearing the right words of reassurance or the healing power of a prayer or mantra. At least as much as the words we say, it is the way we use them which matters.

Behind all of our actions and words the mind is at work. Whether we consider it to reside in the brain or somewhere else is unimportant. What matters is that everything we do or say originates there. Although it is formless and cannot be located precisely, we have to realise that if we wish to improve the quality of our behaviour, it is the mind, ultimately, that has to be dealt with.

As well as being aware of the more obvious manifestations of this troublesome mind, we have also to guard against its subtler, but no less mischievous tendencies. For example, we may

feel that it is quite harmless to watch a violent film or T.V. programme, but if the mind identifies with the torture or killing of
others, unwittingly it may strengthen our disposition to be cruel
and heartless.

Until now it has been a largely selfish, egocentric mind that
has inspired our words and deeds and which, owing to our unwill-
ingness or inability to curb its activity, has known great strength
and power. At the moment we may not even recognise its existence, but at some stage we have to seek out and confront this dicta-
tor, to face up to and deal with the mind on its own level, as it
appears to us now. Then we can say, 'Look, you have ruled my
body and speech for too long. You have caused more than enough
harm and suffering. Now you must be tamed!' Until the selfish
ego-mind is given up or can be transformed there will be no real
progress; but, having achieved this, we can start to move in the
right direction. Meditation can help to allow us the space and time
in which to stand back from the problem and thus see it more
clearly. It can help us begin to understand the mind and how it
works, both in itself and through our body and speech.

We have considered body, speech and mind separately; but
they are, of course, interdependent. For us to make progress on the
path, all three have to make the journey. All three have to be
trained to do fewer of the things which are harmful and disruptive,
and more of the things that are beneficial to ourselves, other
beings and the environment at large.

The exercises in this book are designed to provide a practical
working basis to assist in this endeavour. Later on, as we purify
our body, speech and mind, we can go a little deeper. Then we can
come to understand that they have no real substance or solidness;
that our body is like a rainbow, our speech is like an echo, and our
mind is like a reflection on water. However, this understanding
will not be achieved without a great deal of hard work.

Right Conduct

Right Conduct

To refrain from evil,
Practise perfect virtue
And fully tame one's mind
Is the doctrine of the Buddha.
                                        Gautama Buddha

This is the essence of the teachings of Lord Buddha, complete in itself and relevant to everyone, whatever their level of spiritual understanding. At first sight it is simple advice, but to put it into practice is not so easy, for it is very hard to avoid wrongdoing and to do only positive and virtuous things. In order to tame the mind, a great deal of patience and skill is required. However, we should not be discouraged; the benefits of following this guidance are inestimable. Skilful conduct brings happiness both to oneself and to others; and as long as we try to practise this teaching, we can be sure we are progressing in the right direction.

Everyone wants happiness, but pursuing it may lead us to commit many bad or unskilful acts. For example, in making ourselves happy we might kill other beings, or cheat and steal from them. Unless we know how to behave, we could be creating suffering for others right now, whilst storing up the causes of future suffering for ourselves.

Where do unwholesome actions originate? They arise from

clinging to the notion of a separate ego or self, due to our ignorance. Until now we have held this self very dear, and have
become attached to anything which supports it. Clinging to our
possessions, wealth and pleasurable sensations in turn gives rise
to the development within us of pride, jealousy and greed. Con-
versely, we resent anyone or anything that opposes our view of the
world and our central place in it, so that intolerance, anger and
hatred come into being.

Whereas on a day-to-day level it is practical, even necessary,
to accept the idea of self, on an absolute level, it has no separate
and independent existence. Once we recognise that all phenomena
are conditioned and interdependent, this truth becomes quite obvious.

Ignorance and delusion, then, are at the root of all our
unwholesome actions and create trouble for everyone, whilst the
practice of discipline and virtue increases the quality and value of
our lives. Such practice can help us to meditate, to tame the mind,
whilst freeing us from the stains of previous unwholesome
actions. It can bring happiness both to ourselves and to others.
That is why we need right conduct.

There are various ways of understanding our behaviour, but
one useful method is to regard all virtuous actions as positive and
all non-virtuous actions as negative. We can then see, day by day,
how positive or negative we are. The aim is simply to increase the
positive and reduce the negative, so that eventually everything is
positive. Each morning we should reaffirm the right motivation to
do good and to cause harm to no one. Throughout the day we bear
this in mind, whether we are working, studying or relaxing, alone
or with others. At all times we renew this motivation in everything
we do, say or think. Living with the welfare of others in mind can
bring value and dignity to even the simplest of tasks.

At night, before sleeping, it is useful to recall and examine
our deeds, words and thoughts of that day. If this can be achieved
without self-deception, we can accurately assess our development, with no need to consult anyone else. We will come to recognise negative tendencies and how they arise, so enabling us to
reduce the frequency of their expression. Accordingly, as we learn
to identify the positive and its causes, we can encourage its manifestation in more and more situations. Of course, many of the

things we do are neutral and require no attention.

Our investigation is more than a passive exercise. We don't, for example, merely observe our faults and think, 'I'm a terrible person', or find good points that reinforce our pride and self-esteem. Rather we try to transform or remove what is unwholesome, whilst working to develop and extend the good qualities. By these means, the quality of our lives can be improved. How, then, can we distinguish between the positive and the negative?

According to the Buddhist tradition, right conduct is explained in terms of ten unwholesome and ten wholesome acts, which are based on understanding all activity in terms of body, speech and mind. These guidelines for conduct have been applied and have proven effective for over two thousand five hundred years and are still valid for us today.

We are strongly urged to avoid the ten unwholesome acts. Three of these relate to the body: first, taking the life of any living being; second, stealing, or taking what is not freely given; and third, sexual misconduct – this includes forcing someone against their will or inclination, and causing someone to break their religious vows or commitments within relationships.

Four unwholesome acts relate to speech: it is harmful to mislead or lie to people, or consciously to say what is untrue; second, to speak in such a way as to cause separation or discord between friends or partners; third, to speak ill of others, to denigrate or insult them, or to hurt their feelings by cruelly exposing their faults; lastly, we should avoid saying anything at all which is not useful or beneficial.

The mind is most important. It is the source of all our activity. Thus, if we allow a negative thought to take root now, later on when it has matured and found expression, suffering will certainly result. Three mental tendencies are strictly to be avoided. The first of these is covetousness. This refers to desiring the wealth, possessions or partners of other people. The second is to harbour ill-will towards other beings or to wish them harm in any way whatsoever. Finally, we should never doubt the truth of the law of cause and effect which governs all action, whether wholesome or unwholesome.

It has to be realised that unwholesome actions create only suffering and prevent the attainment of peace and happiness. We don't have to be religious to understand that this is so. If we plant sunflower seeds, sunflowers will grow. If we cause harm to others, their happiness decreases at once and our own happiness will eventually be diminished. To refrain from the ten unwholesome acts automatically produces benefit, but none of us have been completely successful in avoiding them in the past. For this reason, we have to be very careful about what we do, say or think.

We should also try to practise the ten wholesome actions, each of which is the antidote to its opposite. Instead of killing, therefore, we should nurture and preserve life in all its forms. Rather than taking what is not freely given, we should share our own wealth, however limited. Also we should strive always to preserve moral conduct in our relationships.

On the level of speech: we should be truthful and honest at all times; do what we can to repair quarrels and heal rifts between people; speak well of others if we have to speak of them at all; and generally use our speech for helpful and worthwhile purposes.

In our minds we should rejoice at the good fortune of others, rather than thinking, 'If only I had that,' and should always have good will towards them, wishing them happiness. Finally, we should clearly understand and fully accept the truth of the law of cause and effect.

The ten unwholesome and ten wholesome acts represent useful guidelines as to conduct for Buddhists and non-Buddhists alike. Attention to the wholesome will bring about better relations between people, leading to a happier world. If the advice is followed no laws will be broken and no one will be offended. We can be sure that no harm or suffering will result from our actions.

No matter how virtuous is our own conduct, however, we must guard against judging or finding fault in others. Excessive involvement in what others are doing, saying and thinking, or the comparison of their behaviour with our own, may lead to pride on the one hand or discouragement on the other. Instead we do our best to tame our own minds, according to the high standards outlined in the teachings. We look within rather than outside ourselves for signs of progress, or indications as to what still remains to be improved or transformed.

A useful way of measuring our development is to consider our attitude to the faults we perceive in others. The more the mind has been tamed, the fewer faults will be found in others; the more untamed the mind, the more inclined it will be to see faults outside. When our attitude and motivation are genuinely positive, a joyful and wholesome outlook will prevail; but if the motivation is polluted by ignorance and selfishness, our perception will reflect this, and dissatisfaction results. Purity, like beauty, is in the eye and the heart of the beholder.

It is clearly wiser to adapt ourselves to the outside world rather than attempt to make that world conform to our needs and wishes. For example, if the earth's surface were covered with thorns and nettles that made walking difficult, it would be an endless, impossible task to try and hack them all down. If, however, we were to put on a stout pair of shoes, we could comfortably go anywhere, regardless of the thorns and nettles. Similarly once the mind has been tamed, both inner and outer circumstances and situations become easier to accept and to deal with.

Such a radical change in the way we see things will not occur overnight, and we can expect to continue to make mistakes at first. However, this is no reason to get angry, or discouraged, or to punish ourselves. Rather, we maintain a patient, compassionate approach and try to learn from our mistakes. We thoroughly re-educate ourselves so that we can come to deal with difficult situations and relate to other people in a more wholesome and balanced way.

The attitude we adopt when things go wrong is very important. It's easy enough to regard success with equanimity, but failure of any kind provides a far stiffer test. Some people need to be firm with themselves if they are to learn from and prevent the repetition of their mistakes. Others benefit from a gentler, more thoughtful response to having misjudged or mishandled a situation. Clearly, we have to come to know ourselves particularly well if we are to employ the most skilful means in order to develop good qualities through the body, speech and mind.

Further, as one tries to practise right conduct and to transform harmful tendencies, there is a strong possibility that distractions and negative impulses will spontaneously arise. As it is obvious that a bright sun casts a darker shadow than does a hazy or partially-obscured one, we shouldn't be surprised or alarmed if this happens. Rather, we carry on doing the best we can.

On our level then, as beginners, it is useful to recognise that there is positive and negative, good and bad, and that there is a need to discipline the mind. At the end of the path we can transcend these dualistic notions, but in the beginning they do provide material for us to work on, they do indicate the way forward. Later on, as our practice becomes fruitful, the training process can continue without our consciously thinking about it. Then everything we do, say or think will spontaneously and naturally be for the benefit of everyone. It is like learning to drive a car: at first we have to concentrate on every stage of the operation, but after a while we don't have to re-learn everything whenever we want to drive somewhere. Similarly, once we have tamed the mind, the practice of right conduct will come as second nature.

Above all, we should maintain confidence in and respect for the teachings and not abandon them when things become difficult. Their underlying principles are unshakeable, whilst the practical techniques have been refined and authenticated by a hundred generations of practitioners. In short, they can be fully relied upon. It's up to us to integrate these teachings and techniques into our daily lives, to make them our own. Then we will be acting at all times for the benefit of everyone and to the detriment of none. We also will be keeping alive this precious tradition for the benefit of generations yet to come.

Question: Some people feel that if others break the rules of right conduct (and seem to be happy) why shouldn't they as well. Bad people sometimes become very rich and powerful whilst a lot of good people remain poor.

Rinpoche: Maybe the people who cheat become very rich but that does not mean they are happy. The kind of richness that is really worthwhile is living a satisfied life and enjoying or appreciating everything. We can take that kind of richness with us wherever we go, whatever situations we are in. Even if someone is living on the streets in Piccadilly Circus and sleeping in a cardboard box they can still feel rich because of the feeling, 'this is enough for me'. In this situation, also, one has no fear thinking, 'who's going to take away my cardboard box' because it doesn't really matter. To have many houses or cars does not mean you are rich. However, if you practise right conduct and are satisfied in life, this is what can be called richness.

Question: Right conduct is sometimes explained in terms of increasing the number of wholesome actions and putting aside or destroying all negative actions. This is obviously the right way to behave but sometimes when dealing with problems or negativities we are advised not to fight ourselves, or the negativity, but instead to appreciate its quality. Could you clarify these two seemingly different approaches?

Rinpoche: I think one's approach depends on whether one is a beginner, at an intermediate stage, or at an advanced stage. For the beginners, of course, it is necessary to learn how to overcome negative actions. It's no use just to accept them. The mature mind is not there yet. So there is 'negative' and this must be dealt with. To be wholesome in our actions is the first essential stage, the necessary foundation for future development.

The second stage is that when we are able to deal with the negative, we do not just leave it there but are able to recognise and appreciate its qualities. This kind of appreciation is the second stage. The third stage is when our minds are mature and any experience can be integrated into our practice. If we are mature already then maybe we don't have to start at the beginners level. Whatever level we are on, we should think, act and speak in such a way as to benefit people and do them no harm.

COMPASSION

In order to help all living beings in their seemingly unavoidable suffering, we put on the tender armour of compassion, not only for men but for all living entities, seen and unseen.
His Holiness the XVIth Gyalwa Karmapa

Compassion and loving-kindness are essential to our happiness and spiritual development. The problems facing our friends and families as well as those affecting our environment and the world at large can all be helped by these qualities.

The wider and deeper our compassion, the greater and more effective its scope. Thus, if it is truly universal, we are able to care for everyone and everything in the right way. Our family lives become more meaningful and useful and, as our own happiness increases, so more and more others become happier also. Continued growth and expansion of compassion will gradually transform the world for the better, leading to less desire and hatred on a personal level; whilst between nations and groups of people there will be less conflict and fewer wars.

At present a measure of compassion exists in everyone. No matter how selfish people are, they are often still able to care for their parents, children, lovers or friends. Even creatures habituated to killing, such as snakes and crocodiles, maintain affection for their own young. However, when compassion is restricted solely to an individual's immediate family or species, it excludes many more beings than it embraces and is very narrow compared with the limitless compassion which we are all capable of generating. Whereas some compassion is better than none, limitless compassion is the best of all.

In the beginning, it is helpful to realise how we all share the awakened state of mind as potential. However, it has become obscured by ignorance and the accumulation of negativity. Misunderstanding and unskilful actions similarly prevent us from seeing and realising that potential. Removing these obscurations and defilements, however, will enable us to go beyond the illusion of separate existence and realise the interdependence of all things. It will become evident that when we harm others we are harming ourselves; and when we take care of others, we are taking care of ourselves. When we are able to see the awakened state of mind as potential in friend and enemy alike we will have equal compassion for everyone.

Essentially everyone wants happiness and the causes of happiness, just as we do. Even those who create suffering for themselves do so out of ignorance for no-one sincerely wants to be unhappy. They just do not realise that it is virtue that creates happiness and a happy state of mind which inspires us to practise virtue.

First, then, it is necessary to distinguish between wholesome and unwholesome activity. Once we have learned what is right and what is wrong we can begin to apply this knowledge skilfully in our daily lives. The chapter on right conduct provides simple guidelines as to wholesome activity, whilst cautioning against the unwholesome kind, and may be summarised thus: doing good things creates happiness and its causes; unwholesome activities only create further suffering. Unless we can understand this distinction as a foundation for the growth of compassion, we will create unhappiness for ourselves and others whether or not we intend to do so.

Although some people apparently enjoy making themselves and others miserable, they are still in suffering. Often, because of ignorance or habit, or both, they cannot help themselves. A snake may not wish to poison a baby who is playing in the grass but nonetheless does so out of fear and ignorance, even though it's neither hungry nor in danger. For a snake, poison is part of its way of life; for human beings this need not be so. If someone annoys us or does something we deplore, we may grow angry, yet to blame or wish to punish them is not being compassionate at all. We have to learn to avoid reacting harmfully or negatively to others and to guard carefully against striking out at them as might an animal or a snake. In this kind of situation compassion, not anger, is the appropriate response.

To be unkind or selfish is easy for most of us; whilst to be considerate and mindful of others is very difficult. In order to increase our compassion and loving-kindness we try to put ourselves in the place of others and see things from their point of view. So we neither harm others nor do things to them that we would not like to have done to us. Instead we should always try to give others the happiness that we wish to have ourselves. Ultimately there will be no difference between the wish for their happiness and our own. In the social context we can come to fit together like pieces in a jigsaw puzzle. Clearly, to accomplish this we must have considerable awareness of how other people feel.

Compassion and loving-kindness can be developed quite straightforwardly, stage by stage, but this will not occur without a great deal of patient effort on our part. The mind has to be thoroughly trained before compassion can become deep and strong enough to remain intact even when things are going against us. Limitless loving-kindness is our aim.

Although it may be possible to imagine such a wholesome state of mind, we are not there yet. At the moment simply to look after ourselves and not cause harm or be a burden to others may require considerable effort; but if we can accomplish this much we have achieved something very worthwhile. Then we have the right foundation for future growth – for unless we have compassion for ourselves it's very difficult to engender it for others.

To begin with, we must realise how all of us, without exception, are suffering in some way. Rich or poor, gifted or otherwise, we all have to endure the sufferings of birth, old-age, sickness and death. Without liberation we are like prisoners awaiting execution in a dungeon; there is nowhere to run to and nowhere to hide from the inevitability of impermanence and death. No-one wants to suffer and yet we all do so in our various ways, equally unable to escape from that suffering, no matter how hard we try.

Rich people still suffer despite their good fortune: they may live in fear of losing their wealth, or be corrupted by it, or it may lead to the destruction of friendship and trust amongst those they care for. The poor may go hungry, lack shelter, or worry constantly about providing for their loved ones. Intelligent people suffer despite their abilities or even because of them; whereas those less able find simple problems beyond them.

Since all beings are in suffering, whether aware of it and able to admit it or not, our aim is to exclude none of them from the range of our compassion. Having fully realised this, the next stage is to cultivate the strong wish that they be freed from the causes of that suffering.

Limitless compassion is difficult to define but it may be compared to the strength and depth of feeling that exists between a mother and her child, being extended equally to all beings everywhere.

When there are lots of children in a family, in the mother's eyes it may tend to diminish the value of each; but if there is only one child, she cares for it and protects it so that it is happy and comes to no harm. Although there are billions of suffering beings in the world, the ultimate aim is to regard each one as our only child.

In Western society, the parent-child relationship is more distant than in the East. The Western ideal is to give children freedom and independence as soon as possible. Babies are often bottle-fed. Young children sleep apart from their mothers and are often given responsibility before they're ready. They may be left alone while the parents go out to work. Sometimes teenagers go out into the world too early and have bad experiences. This searching for freedom too soon is like house-martins jumping out of their nest too early and then crashing to the ground. Such situations are commonplace and are generally accepted as normal, but in many cases children can even end up in institutions simply because they have too much freedom too soon.

In many places in the East, however, families still follow the tradition of working together and sleeping together. Mothers share their milk as well as their food and happiness with their children, and there is a great deal of closeness, of security between them. Although less common in the West, this kind of loving relationship does represent a good example of deep compassion in action. In this context, another way of developing compassion is to consider how we would feel if our own mother were being tortured or harmed in some way. We might feel, "If only she could be liberated from that suffering." The aim is to engender the same depth of feeling in regard to all beings, to wish fervently that they all could be freed from their suffering. So at the beginning, one practises loving-kindness towards those close to one, such as one's mother, lover or close friend, and then the feeling is expanded and extended to include all beings without distinction.

This is not to say that human beings should be the sole objects of our compassion. Animals also endure great suffering. Many are slaughtered unnecessarily, often without even the justification that they are needed to provide food. Blood sports are practised all over the world; everywhere animals are cruelly exploited by humans, hunted by other animals, and yet still they have to find food and shelter for themselves and their young. It is hard to imagine how a fish feels when it's hooked and dragged from the water, or a fox which is hunted to death, but we can be sure that we wouldn't enjoy such experiences. When a single hair is pulled from our head, we complain or cry out, yet sheep are roughly shorn even during very cold weather. Although we cannot greatly influence the way of the world in these respects, we can strive always to be as kind, gentle and caring as possible towards all forms of sentient life.

Reminding ourselves of how others suffer and mentally putting ourselves in their place, will help awaken our compassion and considerably extend its scope.

The next stage in the development of compassion is to work to liberate all beings from their suffering. The starting-point here is our own suffering, for unless we can confront and deal with those situations which give pain and discomfort to ourselves, we can acquire neither the confidence nor skill necessary to be of much use to others.

In this respect it is important to realise that when we perceive the world and our situation within it in terms of violence or discomfort, then this is our creation – a projection of our own inner negativity. Clearly it would be useless to try to run away, with the intention of finding a better world or some kind of heaven elsewhere. With correct understanding, on the other hand, we can achieve a wholesome, positive relationship with the phenomenal world, here and now.

When our mind is pure, that purity illuminates whatever we perceive, just as someone with good eyesight sees everything clearly, as it is. Defective vision, however, makes everything appear vague and imprecise, giving rise to confusion and misunderstanding. It is useless to try and change the object that is seen – it is the eyesight that has to be improved. If we see negativity in other people, we must try to develop compassion for them and, as our compassion and insight increase, we will stop finding fault in them. Correspondingly, their regard for us will improve, mutual respect will develop and enmity will decrease greatly.

At the moment we try to escape from painful situations, but this achieves nothing. Instead of trying to abandon suffering or pass it on to others, we must recognise its usefulness as a means of developing our fellow-feeling and inner strength.

It is important, however, to remind ourselves that we are not looking for trouble. Quite often people say that suffering is good and that in order to accomplish something worthwhile we should punish ourselves, but this is a mistaken attitude. If our experience presents us with misery or pain then we accept it and use it as a means to develop, but we don't go around actively looking for suffering. The aim is to be flexible and to accept whatever comes our way. Neither should we analyse or dwell too much on the causes of our suffering, for this only magnifies and increases the pain. Simple acceptance is the first step; then we can work with the negative aspects of our experience and transform them into positive ones.

At the same time we have to guard against the notion that because we are practising compassion others must practise it also. We simply get on with the work of developing ourselves and, as our inner happiness and compassion grow, many others will quite naturally become aware of the benefits of what we're trying to achieve, and be inspired, in their own good time, to follow our example.

The aim in developing loving-kindness and compassion is for it to become impartial. We must come to understand that being kind to our friends in preference to our enemies is not the right way. Since a friend of one day can be an enemy the next, and vice versa, we shouldn't take this idea in too solid a way. As far as we can, we treat our enemies as amicably as our friends and see everyone as someone to be kind to.

Of course compassion that is really pure is never a cause of suffering to anyone – like gold, it is immutable and unalloyed. Until we have refined and perfected the practice of compassion, however, we may unintentionally cause a little suffering. Nevertheless we should still go on trying at all times to be helpful.

No matter how many useful things we have learned and taken to heart, the seed of compassion will not grow and become fruitful unless it is exposed to the light of our everyday experience. To study ways of relaxing and to have a broad-minded, caring attitude is of little benefit so long as we're tense and unkind in our daily lives. Were we to buy and feed a 'riding-horse' without ever riding it, the horse could become wild, unhappy and no use to anyone. A horse must be ridden if it is ever to take us where we want to go. Similarly compassion and loving-kindness have to become part of our experience.

Further, the practice of compassion should not be accompanied by any expectation of receiving something in return. To regard one's practice of loving-kindness as some kind of business transaction only reinforces the sense of ego and separate self. Unselfish compassion, however, will expand our horizon beyond the scope afforded by such an isolated, impoverished view of reality and our place in it, so putting us in touch with the essential unity which pervades everything. The right attitude is neither to hope for success nor to fear personal failure but simply, and humbly, to proceed with the liberating effort to care for everyone.

Throughout human history there have been many great saints and masters whose lives were devoted to working hard for the benefit of others. Their achievements were not based on study, the ability to wage war, or on the accumulation of material possessions but on their kindness to all beings. By following their example we too can fulfil the promise of our precious human birth and awaken that limitless compassion in ourselves.

The compassion of the people around us now can also inspire our efforts. There are many honest, sincere and thoughtful people who, for example, send money, food and clothing to families and children in need. When we concern ourselves with the welfare of those less fortunate than ourselves, without pride or desire for fame and recognition, we too will have found the right way. Gradually, as we gain in confidence and strength of purpose, our benevolence can come to include everyone who is suffering – not least those for whom no-one cares and who therefore are most in need of aid and comfort.

This is particularly important in regard to those old and sick people who, in Western society, are so often neglected or put away in homes or institutions. It is quite wrong that the elderly and infirm should be brushed aside like this simply because they are 'in the way' or because they require more care and attention than we feel we can afford. Instead, wherever possible, we should provide that care and support, that security and familiarity which can help them to regard the approach of death as part of the continuity of life – not as something separate, or alien to it.

Of course caring for the old, sick and unlikeable can be very difficult. They often suffer from confusion and irrationality as well as from physical pain and weakness, or they may try to manipulate others in the matter of bequests and legacies. Having enjoyed a greater degree of power and control over their lives than in their old age, it is understandable that they should still wish to influence others by whatever means remain to them.

Although this kind of manipulation is undignified, we should not think ill of those who practise it. In this, as in all things regarding others, we try to put ourselves in their place, to imagine how they must feel, neither condemning nor passing any other kind of judgement. All the time we strive to bring our own minds to maturity, learning from others' mistakes as well as our own, always guided by that limitless compassion which is not only the aim but also the path and the goal.

Unless we understand the right motivation, the practice of kindness and generosity to others could create obstacles. The important thing to remember here is that whatever we are able to give should be given freely, however much or little we have. Reluctance to share one's happiness or possessions is to misunderstand the meaning of compassion. A baby or young child clings to a toy, fearful of losing it. We are like that when we can only think about how to protect a possession and keep it to ourselves. With this attitude, we devalue the possession and no longer find it a source of joy. What we do need to protect at all times is our compassionate motivation. The more we give of ourselves, the stronger and more dependable this will become.

The practice of compassion requires a great deal of skill. For example, to give strong drink to an alcoholic, even if they ask for it, is not being kind at all. Nor should we try to force our help on others or interfere in situations where we can do no good. If we see two people quarrelling, we may think it compassionate to step between them and try to stop the fight. But if this would make them angry with us and we become angry too, then the confusion would only spread and increase. Unless our compassion is deep enough so that we remain in control of our own emotions, even in the midst of anger and conflict, it would be better not to get involved at all.

Therefore whilst always striving to be as helpful as possible, we must guard against going beyond our stage of development. It is no use giving away too much too soon and having regrets and attachments afterwards; instead we are mindful only to give as and when we're ready. Thus the growth of compassion should be steady and gradual. Employing patience, discretion, discrimination and common sense we are able to relate carefully to each situation as it arises, making sure that whatever we do, say or think will cause no harm to anyone and will always be beneficial.

So far we have considered the benefits of loving-kindness and compassion, the way to develop them and how best to practise them. It must be stressed, however, that although the stages of development and practice require patience and careful application, it is never wise to delay the actual awakening of one's compassion and the taming of one's mind.

Generally people wish to enjoy life and be happy, preferring never to think about dying. If we could find worldly enjoyment that would last until the time of our death, there would seem little cause to reconsider this attitude. However, that kind of enjoyment more often lasts only for a short time – a matter of years at the most. Money we accumulate or invest can melt away like ice-cream in the sun; pleasure derived from food or clothing, or from other people's ways of talking or acting, all of these things we cherish are subject to change, so that today's joy and happiness so easily become tomorrow's sorrow and sense of loss. Even during the passage of a single day, a source of pleasure can turn to one of unhappiness.

While there is nothing wrong with enjoying our lives, we should never forget that everything is impermanent, including ourselves, and that our time is far too precious to waste. Although we can be sure that death will come, the time and place of its occurrence is very uncertain. Since we can be sure that at the time of death we would certainly give everything we own for just one more day of life, we should not put off for one moment the awakening of compassion. For when we have to leave all else behind, it is the good we have done that will give us the greatest peace and comfort.

So wherever and whenever we can, we should develop compassion at once. If we leave it until tomorrow then we'll no longer be able to relate so directly to the situation which has inspired that compassion. We don't neglect our hunger and thirst for twenty-four hours, we act immediately to satisfy them. The practice of loving-kindness should be treated with similar urgency, as a natural, spontaneous part of our lives.

Remembering that we are going to die does not suggest that we should live in fear and terror of death, for to become hopeless and afraid would be of no use, and would prevent us from enjoying life. Rather we should be inspired by the inevitability of death to make the most of each precious moment in order to cultivate our inner strength, loving-kindness and compassion. Then, no matter when we are to die, we will have done our best to make of our lives something valuable and useful both for ourselves and for others.

There is no way that we can give up death, but with sufficient effort and the right motivation we can certainly give up suffering. As long as our determination is strong enough and our confidence does not fail, we have the means and the power to neutralise the causes of suffering, to cut them off at source. And if ever we doubt the value of our efforts, we have only to look at our own experience and that of those around us to realise just how worthwhile it is for everyone that compassion should develop and flourish in the world.

Mindfulness

If, when relaxed completely, one observes what happens,
this very act in itself produces strength.
Jetsun Milarepa

Much of the suffering we encounter in our lives is caused by our lack of mindfulness. Every day our ignorance and limited awareness daily give rise to problems and difficult situations. Yet if we are mindful the unwholesome may be positively transformed whilst the wholesome will be neither neglected nor wasted. If we train ourselves in the practice of mindfulness, we find that all situations become easier to deal with, the work that we do becomes more fruitful, and all other aspects of our lives become richer and more worthwhile.

A simple, clear awareness applied to all of our experience, as we are living it, will free us from the emotional errors that are the cause of so much confusion and suffering. So whenever unwholesome tendencies arise and threaten to find expression, we slow down, steady ourselves, and try just to do one thing at a time, thoroughly and completely. That is mindfulness.

We do not need to be religious to see the benefits of mindfulness. It can lead to an increase in worldly as well as spiritual happiness. Whether we are doing visualisation exercises or merely crossing the road, we can use this mindfulness as a basis for our well-being. We can practise it anywhere and at all times while working, eating, riding in a car or enjoying ourselves in the sunshine.

So we are not considering an abstract philosophical concept but something that has to become a practical part of day-to-day existence. Thus it is wrong to think that meditation and mindfulness are activities somehow distinct or different from what we already do, say and think. Rather than trying to find this mindful state outside of our everyday experience, the aim is to integrate it within whatever we are doing, wherever we happen to be.

As we become more mindful of the needs and wishes of others there will be less friction and conflict in our work, at home, and in all of our lives. With mindfulness, we will develop more flexibility and adaptability, together with a better understanding of others and of how they are likely to be affected by the things that we do and say. Presenting ourselves more skilfully, in a less abrasive way, we can co-ordinate our own activities with others.

However, this is no easy task. To transform one's egotistical, selfish attitudes into care and attention for all others requires a great deal of effort. To fit in with others, we must learn how to tame the mind and not harm them by becoming angry, crazy or jealous. Even when we feel bad inside, we should always try to be mindful and not let that negativity hurt others.

Careless and wilful behaviour is often the result of our expressing immediately whatever is going on inside us, not noticing what we are doing. This is not to say we should constantly repress our feelings, for then we might simply create a kind of internal 'rubbish bin' for all our unwholesome reactions. In that case, we could become so full of poison that we'd violently 'vomit' it out and be unable to cope with the results. Instead we learn to regard our thoughts and emotions in a more transparent and less solid manner. Dealing with them in this way will stop the rubbish from accumulating.

Emotional impulses can and will arise, but with mindfulness we can remain calm and avoid acting out their harmful aspects. We simply can pause and be aware of the unwholesome nature and potential consequences of such emotions as anger and jealousy and thereby not be carried away by them. Similarly, if our tendency is to rationalise or justify our negativity and ill-will, we can be aware of our mistake and put a stop to it.

This would appear to be very simple, but this simple way of practice is in fact very difficult because we ourselves have created so many obstacles. In the twentieth century, we have made many machines and invented much new technology, but as a result we have made our lives more complex, rather than simple. Everything we experience, whether we like it or not, is a product of what we have created ourselves, including the busy, active, worldly lives we live. The antidote for what is wrong and too complicated is to simplify everything. How can this be achieved?

First, rather than trying to do several things at once, we attend fully to one thing at a time. We need to live more in the present, right now, instead of always thinking what we might otherwise be doing or what we're going to do next. And we try not to be distracted by the sights, sounds and other sensations going on all around us. As thoughts and feelings arise we simply observe their coming and going in a loose and relaxed manner, without clinging to them. In this way our minds will tend to wander less, to worry less, and be less involved and affected by passing ideas and emotions. This kind of simple, detached awareness enables us to better understand both what we are doing and what is happening around us. Just as a skilled cook can make a nourishing, balanced meal from a few basic ingredients, so we can learn to make the most of what we have already, to do the best we can. Then we won't make the mistake of making our lives more complicated than they already are.

Sitting meditation provides an excellent starting-point for the cultivation of mindfulness. One technique is to simply sit down, relax, do nothing and let our attention turn inwards. We will then be able to see more clearly what is going on in our minds, how confusion arises, and where the mistakes we tend to make have their origin. Generally we are going so fast that we aren't really aware of what is good, what is bad, or where we are going wrong. Just as a film editor runs a film in slow motion, frame by frame, in order to isolate errors and make corrections, so we have to slow down our lives if we want to make adjustments or improvements to the overall picture. As we watch, allowing everything to come and go in its own time, then our thoughts will slow down naturally. We neither reject the bad thoughts, as a censor might, nor do we become fascinated by, or dwell overlong, on what we perceive to be the good ones. We just watch in a non-reacting way. By freeing ourselves from physical activity and from the tendency to act on or react to every impulse that arises, we are able to develop a calm awareness that can eventually pervade all of our experience.

Later on, as our mindfulness develops, we will be able to remain tranquil and undistracted in the busiest and least comfortable of situations, unaffected by the bustle of activity, noise, heat, dust, or even by people who insult or wrong us in some way. At this level nothing can disturb or upset our equanimity. We are peaceful and relaxed at all times and in all situations. Mindfulness has become a pleasurable condition which we can positively enjoy.

We should aim to have peace in our minds. Each of us should take responsibility for what we say, do or think in the way that an ambassador should for the country he represents. To be at peace, we have to cultivate our own selves. If we develop peace inside, it will be no longer something we have to search for outside, and others will benefit from our example. When the mind has fully developed peace, we will not react negatively, no matter what happens.

At the moment, this may seem to be a very difficult task for us, but we should understand that there is nothing in this world that cannot be changed. Since our perception of the environment is conditioned by our own minds, we can overcome all suffering and achieve happiness. We learn neither to run away from the former nor cling to the latter, aware that both states are equally subjective and impermanent. Instead we aim to develop a tranquillity that is beyond ordinary sorrow and joy.

We learn also to rest the mind – not in a dull, half-conscious condition but in one of detached awareness. A good artist sees each detail of a painting as well as the overall picture, so that nothing is missed. At the same time the aim is not only to see clearly and precisely, but also to see beyond appearances and to be aware of the non-solidness of each object.

Everything we encounter and experience through the senses is composed of tiny atoms and sub-atomic particles. When they come together there is form, but since they don't exist separately from the space in which they appear, that form has no genuinely solid existence. Everything is in fact in a state of flux – it can be dissolved, destroyed or re-arranged at any moment. This view of the physical world is substantiated by many recent experiments in the scientific field of particle physics. Exercises like the 'rainbow meditation' later on in this book will help us to see the non-solid nature of things and help us decrease our attachment and involvement with material things.

Mindfulness also will help us to go beyond projecting false ideas and values on to the world around us. Things in the outside world can seem to have their own individual existence, yet it is only we ourselves who are projecting a form or value on to these things. Until our minds are completely pure, our projections can seem to be very solid because we ourselves appear to be very solid. For example, there is not much difference to us between the experiences we have in dreams and those in the waking state; often we feel little difference in the intensity of fear, excitement and other feelings which may arise. When we wake up, however, and realise that we've been dreaming, we can know that these experiences do not have the same significance and consequences that they would in our waking life. In the same way, as the mind develops, the insubstantiality of our waking experiences can be understood. This is why a developed mind is often described as 'awakened' – one that is liberated from the sleep of ignorance and recognises the non-solid nature of all experience.

Another famous example illustrates the power of mental projection, of imagining things. Upon seeing a rope in a dimly-lit room, we may easily think that it's a snake and become afraid. The fear we feel is no different from that which we would experience if it were a real snake. However, as soon as we realise it's only a piece of rope, that fear disappears. This is an example of how everything 'good' or 'bad' is entirely our own projection. There is nothing to cling to or fear other than the values we ourselves attribute to these projections. In this respect, the more real we imagine them to be, the stronger they become.

Everyday experience, even though it seems so solid and real, may be compared to a magic show, a theatrical performance, or a film. If we fail to see this non-solid and dream-like aspect, then we are bound like prisoners by our involvement. Later on, as our awareness develops, we begin to understand how a great many devices, tricks and special effects combine to reinforce the apparent reality of that experience. This understanding could, in a sense, make the show less exciting, but we can still appreciate all its richness, drama and variety. The difference is that we can come to see that all our positive and negative thoughts and feelings are simply the play of the mind. This way we won't be overwhelmed by them nor lose our sense of proportion and perspective. Someone who does not realise the nature of mind will forever be under the spell of illusion. Indeed, it has been said that the difference between enlightenment and non-enlightenment is simply the difference between being able to see and understand and not being able to see and understand.

The freedom to act for the benefit of everyone – to know how most skilfully and appropriately to apply our help – depends largely on the ability to transcend any sense of the world as something fixed, solid and substantial. Once we are free of this limitation, our awareness can increase in range and scope. From a basement, for example, only the very immediate environment can be seen; from a rooftop rather more; whilst from a mountain we can look down on many rooftops. From an aeroplane, however, vast areas and entire countries come into view.

In the same way, the attention and understanding of a wise person are not restricted to his or her own concerns, nor to a rigid, unyielding idea of the world. With detachment and objectivity, situations are seen more clearly, as they are, and there can be mindfulness of everyone's needs and problems. Compassionate awareness like this will enable correct and skilful means to be applied as needed. So our responsibility is to try to increase our awareness, see the whole situation, be willing to help other people with their problems and not to be narrow-minded. This way everyone will benefit.

However, this degree of mindfulness requires diligent maintenance; and our commitment continually has to be reaffirmed. Although difficult, this is by no means beyond our capability. Even now, for example, if we love someone and are about to lose them to someone else, we are able to be aware of our lover's movements and actions every moment of the day. We know who they are with and who they are talking to and can readily visualise each move that they make. Although narrow in its scope, this intense awareness of what's going on does represent a kind of mindfulness. So when we feel we cannot be mindful, we are just being lazy and deceiving ourselves. If our motivation and commitment are strong enough, this awareness and mindfulness can be expanded until it includes all others, not just those to whom we are strongly attached in some way.

To illustrate the process of taming the mind, we may return to the example of training a wild horse. To train a horse requires a great deal of care. If we imprison or get angry with it, a horse will become restless, neurotic or rebellious, and we will probably do more harm than good. It might even become untameable. The right approach is to be kind, gentle and patient, allowing it to run free from time to time, but not excessively. The horse will respond favourably to such sympathetic handling. It will learn to trust us and will come back to us when called, since we are both firm and fair, as necessary, and consistent without being so rigid as to deny its natural spontaneity. To tame either a horse or our mind we must first make friends with it. In this respect both compassion and mindfulness are vital.

How, then, should we react when we feel we are not being mindful or that we are unable to meditate as calmly and peacefully as we would like? First, there is no need to panic. In the deepest sense, there are no good thoughts or bad thoughts and our moods and mental states are a lot less solid and fixed than they seem. Nor should we over-react if too many thoughts and feelings arise and cause confusion or uncertainty. Instead, we try to relax and simply observe the play of the mind. However, if we're trying to visualise something in particular, or are purposely attempting to develop a specific quality – such as compassion – then the wandering or unruly mind should gently be brought back to the subject.

In daily life, rather than getting too involved in what's going on in our mind, we should pay more attention to where we are and what we're doing at any given time. We do encourage the mind to run in the right direction, but we don't try to force anything. Reins enable a rider to be aware of and influence a horse's movements, and to apply a little guidance where necessary. But if the rider pulls too hard, the horse may fight back. So at all times we aim for a balance between repressing the mind and giving it too much freedom. We learn to experience our thoughts in an accepting, uncontrived way; neither being too tense nor too loose. Thus our meditation and practice of mindfulness follows the wide and safe path – the middle way.

The mind is a very fertile ground. What is planted there is

likely to grow and eventually to bear fruit. If, whilst sitting in meditation postures, we get involved in thinking negatively of other people, then our attitude towards them in daily life will be conditioned and adversely affected by this. Such tendencies reflect an uncontrolled mind and could be very harmful. Since our aim is to engender and cultivate the awakened state of mind, we must be mindful that our practice does not compromise or violate this intention.

It is easy enough to recognise what is ugly or wrong in our thoughts, but when we try to transform these impurities there is a strong tendency for our minds to revert to the way they were before. Thus, when we use visualisation or other practices, even though there may be good progress initially, our habitual tendencies continue to exert a powerful influence. In this respect the mind has very elastic properties: we stretch it a little, let go, and it springs back again. Just as we would nail down a length of elastic to prevent this happening, we have to apply strong discipline in the process of training the mind, so that when we do encounter difficult circumstances we avoid reacting in habitual, negative ways and instead preserve our good intentions.

These difficulties can in fact be very useful. As well as deepening our understanding of how the mind works, they also serve to expose weaknesses we may prefer to ignore, whilst reminding us of the work that still has to be accomplished. Gradually, as we persist in our practice, new, wholesome tendencies will become as habitual as were the old, unwholesome ones, until eventually the negative will be outweighed and effectively neutralised by the positive.

So when we encounter obstacles it is no use going to sleep and hoping they will have disappeared, as if by magic, by the time we wake up. That would be to ignore a clear indication that we need to look more deeply into ourselves. We may not want to, but we need to do so in order to develop. Since babyhood we have striven to ignore or forget the unwholesome side of ourselves, whilst playing up our good, truthful and attractive qualities for all, if not more than, they are worth. So, it is wise to face up to what is wrong with ourselves and change accordingly.

As well as being honest with ourselves, we also have to be patient. It has taken us a long time to become what we are now and any change for the better cannot be expected to occur overnight. All of us make mistakes until we have gone beyond doing so. Our aim is to use both the positive and negative sides of our experience for our development. Spiritual growth is fuelled as much by the negative as the positive aspects of experience, just as a fire burns equally well whether it is fed with wood, expensive incense, or unwanted rubbish.

Within us is the potential to be whatever we choose. If we wish for a peaceful, worthwhile existence, benefitting all others as well as ourselves, this is certainly within our capability. The first step towards achieving this aim is to simplify our lives so that everything we experience becomes an opportunity to practise mindfulness, rather than a source of confusion. Such basic activities as the way we sit, stand, walk and talk, as well as our attitude to cleanliness and tidiness, are easy to neglect, and yet so fundamental that they condition all other activities.

All the time, whether anyone is watching or not, we should be aware of what is going on inside us and guard against being careless or unmindful in our daily lives. That way we will not harm others. The aim is gradually to develop mindfulness and activate that compassion and loving-kindness which is within us already. This is something we are all capable of doing.

The Exercises

Introduction

Hasten slowly, you will soon arrive.
                              Jetsun Milarepa

The second part of this book is a practical manual for developing the mind so that we are able to put to use the advice in the first part. It is made up of a series of exercises to help people bring their minds to a state of compassion and maturity. Some of the exercises deal with suffering, negative emotions and enemies; situations we would normally prefer to avoid. Yet, if we learn to face such situations then, gradually, what is painful can be confronted and dealt with properly.

From birth onwards we have acquired many bad habits that cause suffering. We have been conditioned to believe in the value of a strong ego and to use the better part of our energy to enhance and satisfy it. At school, we are taught how to act and react, what to say and what to see as right and wrong. We are conditioned by our parents and society to behave in certain patterns and to look at things the same way that they do.

Much of our early training is useful, and through the right sort of analysis we will come to see clearly which parts we want to keep and which are not necessary. We will identify the causes of our bad habits and have the opportunity to correct the mistakes of body, speech and mind which we have been making since we were young. By taking these teachings to heart, we may re-educate ourselves to develop more compassion and understanding. Thus, the value and usefulness of our lives will increase.

The pressured pace of life in Western society causes particular difficulties in our lives. We do not have time to digest things fully or the distance to see things clearly. We get too involved with our own affairs and store up problems instead of dealing with them as they arise.

It is not pleasant to face pain or difficulties, but we should not always try to avoid them. We can create a lot of suffering by trying to enjoy ourselves all of the time, as this is an impossible goal. Any pleasant thing taken to excess breeds suffering. For example, for the person who loves good food and cannot resist eating it when it's there, eating becomes like a disease. We must also overcome the opposite extreme of always trying to avoid or reject things with the feelings, 'I don't want to do this,' 'this is their problem, not mine,' or 'I don't want to be with that person.' What we are aiming to do is to go beyond the extremes of over-enjoyment and over-rejection and bring genuine balance into our lives.

The tendency to over-react when things go right or wrong brings suffering to ourselves and others involved with us. Thus our minds need training, so that we may find balance and stability whatever the outer circumstances. It is like training a horse that is frightened by the sound of fire. By gradually acquainting the horse with the noise of fire, he will no longer be surprised by it and will cease to panic when he hears it. Similarly, if in meditation exercises we confront anger and pain again and again, over a period of time, we will be able to face and deal with them in life.

Yet through these exercises we can try to create a space for ourselves which allows us more understanding of difficult situations and how to deal with them even as they are happening. For example, the coloured light visualisations will help us learn to deal with the negative emotions which often overpower us.

The friend/enemy meditations will help to free us from solid ideas we have about who is a friend and who is an enemy. Often one who acts as our enemy can be the best person to teach us how to develop patience and compassion. Our so-called friends, on the other hand, can hold us back from inner development by encouraging our attachment and by being too possessive towards us.

This sequence of techniques for training the mind can be seen as a kind of therapy. 'Therapy' is something which may seem strange to us now, but it is really something very ordinary. Everything we do can be therapeutic. The food we eat, the clothing we wear, the colours we choose to have around us, the sounds we make can all be like medicine and have a healing quality. Conscious 'therapy' is necessary when we have lost our basic naturalness and forgotten our instinctive humanity. Through too much study and education we may lose touch with our lives, our friends and our bodies. Therapy is not something only for the sick. Nor do we have to be ashamed of our interest in it. It can help us all to live more balanced and useful lives.

Meditation is not something altogether new to us either. A broad definition of meditation can include any type of relaxation. Looking from this perspective, all humans and animals meditate, but generally are not aware that they do and are thus ignorant of how to develop it.

Sitting down to a cup of tea when we have been working hard physically and are thirsty is both satisfying and relaxing. We could see this as 'therapy' or 'meditation'. However, if we sit around all day compulsively drinking cup after cup, the twentieth cup will be neither beneficial nor relaxing and could even be harmful.

Amongst Western people today there is much mental suffering due to too much physical freedom. We don't have physical work we have to do, so many of us do less and less and worry more and more. A feeling for therapy, in the sense of following the natural human instinct for balancing body and mind together, throughout each day, will improve our experience and outlook. A right understanding and practice of meditation – a moment-to-moment awareness of all we do, say, feel and think – will bring deep and lasting benefit.

In using these exercises we should recognise that everything changes constantly and that no book can meet the varied and shifting requirements of all its individual readers. That is the limitation of a book. However, these techniques outline a general and logical path to help the mind grow and become more mature while learning how to overcome difficulties. Whenever we try to achieve something worthwhile there can be problems. Sometimes we will encounter strong feelings not to practise for days at a time or to abandon practice altogether. Although there is no value in forcing ourselves to do things, we must try to discipline our minds. This should not be seen as a loss of freedom, but rather as a method for working our way out from under the control of negative emotions. In this way we may enjoy more freedom in our lives.

Sometimes when we want to do therapy exercises or meditation, we can find that we are in a disturbed state of mind. In that case, any attempt at relaxation may just increase our agitation, despair or whatever negative state of mind is dominating at the time. At these times it may be more helpful to do something physical – like go for a brisk walk, work in the garden or get down to some neglected household task. It is very important to work with ourselves in a natural and down-to-earth way and not lose our common sense.

It is wise to go through the whole sequence one by one, doing each properly before going on to the next. Done like this there will be no problem. The experience of each exercise will change and develop as you go along. Each step is valid. To get the full benefit, we should see that together they make a unity, just as the hands, arms, legs, head, torso etc. make a complete body. None of the exercises should be left out simply for the sake of preference. If we try just a few of the exercises we think we might like we won't get the full benefit.

These practices will repay the amount of time and attention put into them. However busy we are, we can find time if we really want to find it. Once we realise their value, we will learn to make the time, in the way that early morning joggers do. Regular drinkers always find time to go out to the pub, so we can easily find time to train and develop our minds. Without being fanatical, the more we give, the more we will achieve. However, some practice is better than none at all. Even to read through the instructions will be of some value and may lead to their being practised or understood later on.

As we progress through the exercises, if some go well and others not so well, we should not worry about it. As long as we do our best, without fixed expectations, it is alright. When difficulties arise, we should not be discouraged, but should make an effort to overcome them. However, if there is any strong feeling of fighting either oneself or the exercise, then take one or two days' rest before going on. If we try to force ourselves too much, we could do more harm than good. It is better to attempt to do the practice when the mind is less tense, and to use the first three 'relaxing', 'feeling', and 'openness' exercises to help us when any of the others become too difficult.

If many thoughts arise while doing the exercises, we should not worry about them, but simply relax and return to the focus of meditation as soon as we notice the distraction. If necessary we can take a little break, or do the relaxing exercises, before we try again. It is up to us to discover whether we are being too hard or too soft on ourselves. We should take a middle way.

Many of the practices use visualisations of the sphere of golden light. In this context we can understand the sphere not as a simple form but as the embodiment of overcoming the negativities of the mind and arriving at a stage of universal compassion and total awakeness. But if there is any religious or intellectual resistance, or any discomfort caused by using the sphere, we can imagine instead the essence of universal compassion appearing as the Buddha or Christ, or whoever embodies the qualities outlined above.

The meditations given here are not meant to achieve something extraordinary, but simply to help us to face the variety of situations which arise every day of our lives. To appreciate our development, we can look to see how we are dealing with these situations. If facing difficult situations is becoming easier, then we are doing well. However, we must be patient in our approach, and not look for instant results, but realise that it is difficult to overcome the deep habits of ego-clinging. It will help us to remember that what we are doing is not just for ourselves nor just for now, but for the good of everyone and for all of our futures. No matter how slowly we may be travelling, we can be confident we are moving in the right direction.

Throughout all the exercises, it is very worthwhile to learn how to relax and simply accept whatever it is that we are feeling. A relaxed mind is a good basis for developing maturity and stability.

If even after patient practice things are not going so well in facing oneself and daily situations, then one could try to find some guidance from a good teacher, or the support of a group. However, it is wise to investigate the organisation or teacher before putting confidence in them. It is also possible to write to Akong Rinpoche, at Samyé Ling.

Many of the difficulties that arise may be resolved (for some people) by doing 'Back to Beginnings'. This is a process of reviewing one's whole life in depth and detail as slowly as necessary in order to face memories and see the present implications of past experiences. It involves eighteen months of sifting and making sense of one's life experiences from the present back until the age of one, then forward again to the present time and then back again to the age of one week. After this there follows an exploration of the phase of life from conception through to birth. There seems to be a magnetic attraction or repulsion to the idea of birth. However in this therapy where seventy-five weeks are spent on understanding one's life since birth, and one week understanding one's life before and during birth one can hardly call it rebirthing. Its value is in seeing how we are creating the future even as we are acted upon by the past. In other words, the birth experience is no big deal. It is more like a ritual for leaving behind bad habits from the past.

In this context there is a key phrase – 'Compassion through Understanding'. Compassion for oneself and compassion for others is involved. Particularly difficult is that part of the process known as clarifying blame (*Back to Beginnings* booklet), which most people leap over and wish to avoid. This exercise is done when a memory brings up angry feelings. After you have got the anger and blame out into the open, you put yourself, to the best of your ability, in the place of the person you were angry with and try to see it from their point of view, as they would have seen it at the time. As you get an understanding of what was happening with that person, how they were, you cannot remain angry, the anger and suffering dissolve. A reconciliation takes place inside your own heart and then you do not have to carry the burden of resentment any more.

Another therapy programme that has helped some people with the 'Taming the Tiger' exercises is 'Working with the Elements'. The five elements – earth, water, fire, air and space – are very important. The beauty of this method is also that it is very simple. You can relate what is going on inside you to what is going on outside – to natural laws being out of balance in yourself as they relate to being out of balance in nature. There is a lot of awareness at the moment of 'Green' issues, but if our inner ecology is out of balance we will be adding to the pollution too. We are made of these five elements ourselves, after all.

Once we have completed the full sequence, any and all of the techniques may be used to overcome weaknesses and obstacles that may arise. Apply each technique as seems appropriate and useful. The sequence of practices is designed to allow those interested in a spiritual path to begin serious and effective meditation, relatively free from the obstacles created by negative states of mind.

We should try to put to use the kind of understanding we develop through doing the exercises. It is no use to sit comfortably in meditation on compassion for an hour and then come out and start quarrelling. The teachings should become like our skin – never separate from us. Whatever we understand or achieve, we must learn to share for the benefit of everyone. It will help us if we consciously share the good results of our practice at the end of each session. We should think in this way:

Whatever good understanding or positive mind we have achieved, may we apply this in our lives and share it with everybody, especially those who are suffering, either physically or mentally. By the power of universal truth, rather than by any power of our own, may all beings overcome their suffering or at least be able to face it. May they all become happy.

Question: In doing the exercises should we guard against setting too high a goal?
Rinpoche: Too much expectation of results is not useful – something is forced. The purpose of the exercises is that they should become part of a way of life, not change black into white overnight.

Question: When you talk of a strong ego which is strengthened by education, is this the same thing as a strong sense of identity? And is there anything good to be said for the ego? Don't we need it in order to go about our business in the world?
Rinpoche: I think we do need a certain kind of objective ego, some sense that, 'I must go in this direction; I have to achieve this.' But when that stage has been reached, we have to be willing to abandon that ego rather than carry on clinging to it – just as we

throw away a pair of shoes when they're worn out. So the right kind of ego is necessary at the beginning; but once the desired change has been achieved, we don't need it any more – not any form of ego.

Question: If someone doesn't want to visualise the sphere of golden light for some reason, is it alright to visualise Buddha, Jesus or some other great teacher one has faith in?
Rinpoche: Yes, certainly. When we talk about a Buddha it means one who has all the qualities of a Buddha, who is totally awakened and purified, with dedication and limitless compassion. So whatever form someone considers as embodying all these qualities, then this is alright. Whatever one can relate best to in order to develop wisdom and compassion, that is the one which will be most effective.

Question: If the exercises are done regularly for a while and then for some reason we stop doing them for weeks or months, is it better to start again from the beginning or to carry on from where we stopped?
Rinpoche: That depends how beneficial you have found the exercises. If the completed exercises provided full benefit then it may be possible to carry on from where you left off; but if you didn't get the full benefit of the exercises then you may have to start again.

Question: How can one avoid falling into traps – like becoming proud of one's achievement, or any other distorted attitude towards the practice? I mean if the practice is done by the book, without a teacher, is it possible, while doing the exercises, to develop in a negative way?
Rinpoche: If you've never analysed yourself, and ever since you were born you've carried around this projected image of yourself, it could be that your projection, your opinion of yourself is quite inaccurate – particularly if no one has ever told you whether that self-image is the right or wrong one. You might think, 'I am the Power of Light', or some such. This could be a big mistake. So

it's very helpful when other people tell us, 'You're not so good, so beautiful or so wonderful as you think,' because it prevents us believing in, and becoming like, that false image we're projecting. In the same way a teacher can prevent us falling into that trap by dispelling our illusions and guiding us in the right direction. So, yes, going entirely by the book can be misleading if we interpret it solely in terms of our self-image – there wouldn't be much use in that approach.

Question: So if you are not in contact with a teacher, what's the best way to avoid these difficulties?
Rinpoche: You just try to develop compassion as much as possible and be guided by that – until you do meet someone who knows about this approach.

Question: If negative emotions and problems come up, is that always a sign of wrong practice; or could it be an effect of the therapy, of unconscious tendencies emerging?
Rinpoche: That's difficult to say – it could be either, or both. Negative emotions may have been there all along but, because of unawareness, you didn't realise you had them. If you've always put too much value on yourself, seeing only the side you want to see, then when you start to analyse yourself suddenly the negative emotions, the other side becomes apparent. This may not be very encouraging – but anyway, whether it's a good or a bad thing, as long as you don't take any emotions too seriously, but simply remain aware of your thoughts and emotions, then I don't think there will be any lasting difficulty.

Question: These days all kinds of people offer all sorts of therapy. Would you say these are generally useful, and in which respects do they differ from your Buddhist approach?
Rinpoche: I'm not able to speak on behalf of other people, but I'm sure many people provide therapy that is useful to others, and this can only be for the good. Others may be less successful, and some harm may be caused. It very much depends on the therapist's

motivation, as of course the influence of the therapist has a great effect on the therapy itself. So it depends how experienced the therapist is, or whether someone has simply invented procedures because they haven't anything else to offer and have no tradition to rely on. The Buddhist idea of therapy is based on the mental approach, on how to tame one's mind. Whoever has personal knowledge of how to tame the mind is suitably qualified to help others to do so.

Question: How can I strengthen my motivation, my wish to practise? I have a strong conviction that it's necessary, but laziness and mental blocks are always getting in the way.
Rinpoche: I think the important thing is to do the very best you can at any given time, rather than waiting until you become a perfect human being. Through helping other people you are helping yourself. Even if mistakes are made, one can learn from them, and through those mistakes one can better learn how to take care of oneself. It's better to give whatever help you can, to base the practice on helping whoever needs that help, than to go around saying, 'I want to help you, but I'm not really ready yet to do so.'

Question: What's the difference, or relationship, between therapy and meditation?
Rinpoche: Therapy and meditation are not so dissimilar. As I've said, therapy means to heal. If you cut a finger, then to put a plaster on that cut is therapy; at the same time you learn not to cut it next time. Physical therapy benefits the physical side of one's being; whilst any therapy related to the mind is a kind of meditation.

Question: So, in effect, anyone who meditates properly is also doing therapy?
Rinpoche: Yes. Not only that, but eating food, sleeping, wearing clothes, relaxing – whatever a person needs, that's therapy.

Question: What does being compassionate really mean?

Rinpoche: My idea of being compassionate is to let everyone become part of one's life. It is to know that everyone wants happiness, just as I want happiness; and that no-one wants suffering and unhappiness. The trouble is that, due to ignorance, we don't know how to be happy, so we tend to have lots of unhappy experiences. Compassion means to be willing to help everyone equally, whether or not they are useful to me; whether they are angry or violent towards me; even if they wrongly accuse me of something. Whatever experience people give me in that way only increases the wish to help; but there should be no expectation as to the outcome, the result of that help. So if, for example, your helping someone gets you sent to prison, you learn to be thankful that you're able to take away that person's negative emotions and exchange them for your own happiness. That's genuine compassion – when you give whatever you have without expecting anything in return.

Question: In your travels, what are the most common cross-cultural problems?
Rinpoche: The problems that people face do differ a lot from country to country, but the most common of all is a kind of impatience with the process. Very few people have a feeling for sticking with a process long enough to make their efforts come to some fruition.

Sustained effort is something very difficult for people in the West, or for people who come from a European background. The prevailing attitude in most Western cultures is to expect results very quickly. The timespan between input and result is becoming shorter and shorter. Many, many people are not willing to invest the time in their own deep benefit. They just want something that makes them feel better about themselves NOW, and that is a big obstacle to the process.

Question: You say at one stage that when practising these exercises we can be confident we're moving in the right direction. What exactly do you mean? I mean, what signs of real progress should we be looking for?
Rinpoche: I think that if in doing the exercises you find it a little

easier to deal with the situations of everyday life, then that's useful progress. If you're doing them properly, you're not so likely to create further problems, or fall so easily into negative situations. Instead, something good will come of the practice – it will bring you to being a proper human being.

Timetable

1. **Posture** – a few minutes before each session, then as needed
2. **Relaxing** – 15 minutes a day for four days
3. **Feeling** – 1 hour a day for 1 week
4. **The Golden Light of Universal Compassion** – 20 minutes a day for 2 weeks.
5. **The Rainbow** – 1 hour a day for 1 week
6. **The Mirror**
   Phase 1 – 15-20 minutes once or twice daily – minimum 1 week. Suggested time three to four weeks.
   Phase 2 – 15-20 minutes once or twice daily for 3 or 4 weeks
7. **The Friend** – 45 minutes a day for 3 to 4 weeks
8. **Awakening our Potential** – 1 hour and 45 minutes a day for 1 week
9. **Bringing the Potential to Life** – 1 hour and 15 minutes a day for 4 weeks
10. **Expanding and Contracting** – 1 hour a day for 3 weeks–
11. **The Enemy** – 1 hour and 20 minutes a day for 4 weeks
12. **Taking Suffering from Parents and Relatives** – 1 hour and 15 minutes a day for 2 weeks
13. **Taking Suffering from our Country, Friends and Animals** – 1 hour and 15 minutes a day for 2 weeks
14. **Taking Suffering from Enemies** – 1 hour and 30 minutes a day for 4 weeks
15. **The Rainbow Sphere** – 1 hour a day, giving one week for each colour
16. **Universal Compassion** – 30 minutes a day for 4 weeks
17. **Universe Transformed by Compassion** – 30 minutes a day for four weeks

The times suggested for the exercises are given in order for there to be the greatest benefit for each of them and for the sequence as a whole. However, it is recognised that not everyone will be able to fulfil these times. There are some who will find they only can manage about half an hour a day and will wonder if they should undertake the sequence at all. Others may find that they have the time, but not the patience or discipline to do the full time suggested and may wonder if these exercises are only for those who are already mature. In both of these cases some is better than none and everyone can do their best. It is advised however that you make a commitment, however short, for a certain period each day. You may, perhaps, want to do two or more shorter sessions, but whatever you decide, it is important to make a commitment and stick to it as best you can. The number of days given is the minimum which should be spent on each exercise. To do less because you do not like this or that particular exercise may deprive you of understanding its purpose.

Some may want to do the exercises just as they please. This will bring the benefit of each individual exercise but to have the full long-lasting value one should keep to the time and sequences given. It really depends on how much one wishes to benefit from them – one will only get out what one manages to put in.

One may wish to do more than the time suggested. If there is the opportunity, this is alright. However, at the end of each exercise, you must achieve at least the minimum recommended times in order to have a good result.

Before beginning each exercise it is useful to spend a few minutes establishing the situation. One may follow a formula like:

'Find yourself a comfortable sitting position with your spine upright. Feel the space around you, where you are and become aware of the sensations of the body as it is resting on the ground. Be aware of the breath as it comes in and out of the body – do relaxation breathing exercises if necessary and then start the exercise.'

At the end of each exercise try to remember to share the positive results of the practice using the 'dedication' given in the introduction to the second section.

After one has gone through the exercises in the book, one may find it useful to return to one or more of them that have been especially helpful. This is fine. However it is wise when working through the exercises the first time to keep to the sequence given. In this context, it is also beneficial to keep to the proportions of the times given within each exercise e.g. 'Awakening our Potential' should be one hour and forty-five minutes but if one cannot do all that time, then still the relaxation phase at the end should be in proportion to the time of the main visualisation.

Question: We are being told to make a regular commitment but for some of us the whole problem is being unable to make such a commitment anyway. What should we do?
Rinpoche: This inability should not be an excuse for not carrying on with the work of 'Taming the Tiger'. This may be your special problem but the important thing is to keep on going and always do your best.

Question: Is it alright to do longer times for the exercises if one feels it to be useful?
Rinpoche: Yes, that is O.K. The only exception is the mirror exercise. In that case we should not do too long a session because of the unusual visual effects that can arise from looking into a mirror for too long a time. If these visual effects happen even in shorter sessions, then make the sessions shorter still. The purpose of the exercise is to see yourself more clearly as you really are – not to get involved in strange visual effects.

Question: I find many of the exercises difficult because I have a short attention span. How can I work with this?
Rinpoche: First of all it is useful to remember that these exercises will be of benefit for the rest of your life – this will help encourage you to do your best. If your attention span is short, and you cannot follow the suggested times, then make a shorter time to begin with and then add a little more every two or three days. Increase the time gradually until it is the same as suggested in the book. That way you will be able to have the full benefit.

Question: Is it alright to split the times of the longer exercises into two sessions daily?

Rinpoche: This can be done. However it takes some time for the mind to settle down so ten or fifteen minutes must be added to each of the two sessions to allow for this.

1. Posture

We sit down to do these exercises or to meditate in order to help us tame the mind and find inner peace, but how should we best go about it? First of all, the environment is important. For beginners especially it is best to try and find a quiet place, free of distracting noises like talking or laughter, but natural noises like running water or birdsong are alright; especially if they give a relaxed feeling.

If we are sitting outdoors, then the countryside and other quiet places are good. It is especially good to sit at the top of a hill from which we can see a long way. Alternatively, to be by the calm ocean with no visual distractions is also very good. Often we do not have the opportunity to be in such places, but then we must try and find the quietest surroundings that we can.

If we are sitting indoors, the room should be as free as possible from distractions, and well-ventilated, not stuffy. The temperature should not be so cold that we shiver, nor so warm that we feel sleepy and dull. Generally, it is better for it to be a little cold rather than too warm, so that the mind is clear.

Once we have found the best environment for our practice, it is important to learn how to sit properly. The postures we use can affect how we feel in our meditation and our day-to-day life. If we look at it from a medical viewpoint, we can see that the body has arteries, veins and muscles, each connected to the organs. In the Tibetan and Chinese systems of healing these organs can be diagnosed and treated by putting pressure on particular parts of the hands, neck or feet. This is because of the meridians, the channels by which energies flow throughout the body.

When sitting, if we are careful not to block the flow of these energies, then they can flow freely without our becoming too uncomfortable or doing any harm to our body. We can see how, if an artery in one leg is blocked, then that leg will go to sleep. Similarly, a blockage in the flow of energy through the body while sitting will produce unhappy, unbalanced feelings. For example, some bad positions will feel good to begin with but after a few days may well produce feelings of depression. Other wrong positions, like having our head sunk down between our shoulders, might bring depression to begin with but later, after the session is over, an uncontrollable excitement may arise. Further, if we use angry words to our relatives and friends after doing the exercises, then our posture could be responsible.

However, some might disagree and prefer their own way of sitting because of the powerful experiences and emotions which arise, such as joy or anger. But we have enough of these kinds of extreme feelings already without needing to cultivate them further. So in doing these exercises we try to sit in a neutral, balanced way.

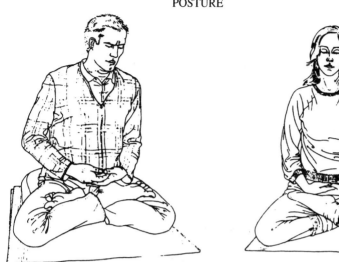

First of all, it is important, if possible, to sit in a cross-legged posture. The Lotus and Semi-Lotus postures are best. This is because they help one to sit for long periods with the spine erect and also help keep energies flowing self-containedly in the body. However, if we are not able to sit in them due, for example, to leg trouble or the stiffness of growing older, there is no need to try and break our legs. Sitting cross-legged is comfortable for most people and is quite acceptable. Otherwise, we can just sit in a chair. If we are young, however, and have no physical disability then it is useful to learn how to sit in the different versions of the cross-legged positions.

Either in the Lotus or Semi-Lotus position, we always put the left leg inside and the right leg outside. The left is folded first, followed by the right leg. With the full Lotus posture, one puts the left foot and ankle up on the right thigh and then puts the right foot and ankle up on the left thigh. In the Semi-Lotus position, the left foot is drawn in with the heel pointing towards the base of the spine and then the right leg is drawn in with the heel placed above the other one. Remember, however, to go cautiously if there is any difficulty with these.

Then we should try to straighten our backbone as much as possible up to our neck. This is partly because each organ in the body is connected through the nervous system to the spine. So if the spine is bent or out of place, then it can cause pain or discomfort in other parts of the body. When we straighten our backbone, our energies can flow freely. Our bodies should feel balanced, with the shoulders straight but relaxed, not forced back, and not higher on one side than the other.

In order to straighten the spine and keep it erect, we should use a small, hard cushion two to four inches in thickness and about twelve to fourteen inches square, depending on what is a comfortable position for us. If we are sitting in a Lotus position we should use a higher cushion (about four inches) as necessary. If crossing one or two legs over is too uncomfortable, then we may sit in the same way, but with the legs loosely crossed. Another possibility, which is comfortable for some, is kneeling supported by a low stool (sometimes called the Burmese posture with the legs tucked underneath the torso) or supported by cushions either way so that the back is balanced and straight.

There are two positions for the hands. We may rest the hands palms down on the knees with the elbows straightened; alternatively, we can rest the open right hand on top of the open left hand with the thumbs touching, but not pressing, and have the hands one and a half inches below the navel. In this second position, we should try not to have the hands resting too low or too high. The

neck should be very slightly inclined, with the chin tucked inwards. The mouth should be slightly open with the tongue touching the roof of the mouth. In this way we can breathe through the mouth and the nostrils together in whatever position is comfortable.

Our eyes should be looking forward beyond the top of our nostrils, about one and a half to two yards in front of us. For beginners it is probably wiser not to close the eyes. However the eyes maybe closed if we are visualising something. We should remove glasses and not focus the eyes in an artificial way.

All of this might sound difficult and uncomfortable, but it is necessary to do the best we can, as long as we do not make ourselves too tense or give ourselves too much pain. If there is a strong resistance to sitting in this way, or there is much tension, the three relaxing exercises at the beginning of the series may be done lying down on the back – but paying attention to the position of the spine, taking care that it is as straight as possible. As in the sitting posture, the chin should be slightly tucked in, so a small book, cushion or folded blanket may be placed under the head, as necessary. If you have pain in the lower back, then it is good to

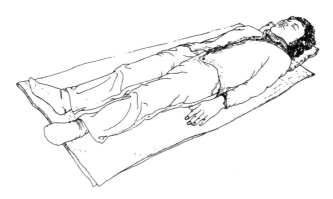

place cushions under the knees until the lumbar area is perfectly comfortable. However, once the exercises are familiar and there is sufficient ease in approaching them, it would be good to try them again while sitting in whatever posture can be managed easily.

The position of the body is important. The idea is not to hold our body inside a rigid frame or chain it with pieces of iron like a prisoner. A relaxed way is better. For example, we can think of cotton wool. It is very loose and relaxed, while at the same time all the fibres are separate. They are together but in a loose way. Similarly, our posture should be balanced: neither too loose nor too tight. With practice, this will help our minds to be balanced also.

Question: Why is the cross-legged posture preferable to kneeling with the support of a bench or a cushion?
Rinpoche: In general, sitting cross-legged is more beneficial for the mind; but for those unable to sit that way then kneeling would certainly not be harmful.

Question: So if the legs are very tight and the knees stick up in the air when sitting cross-legged, should we persist in trying to sit this way? And if so, what advice can you give which will make it easier to do so properly?
Rinpoche: Yes, it would be useful to try a little physical training in order to achieve the ideal position. Different people have different problems in this respect, but in general regular exercises – stretching and so on – should be helpful, as well as regular massage. The important thing is not to try too hard, not to force anything.

Question: Rinpoche, do you feel it's significant that, as Westerners, over many generations we've become so used to using chairs?
Rinpoche: I wouldn't know exactly. Maybe it's a sign of restlessness, of being ready at any time to get up and move to somewhere else. Or it could be laziness – when you're halfway up and halfway down you don't need so much energy to go either more up or more down. But I'm only guessing.

Question: I find it easier to sit cross-legged when my right leg is tucked under the left one, rather than the other way round. Is this okay?

Rinpoche: It very much depends how far your therapy goes: if it's purely physical then it may not be so important; but if the aim is to practise meditation, too, then it would probably be more useful to try and learn the way that is suggested. So although in the beginning it may not really matter, a little courage now could be more beneficial in the long run.

Question: Why are the people illustrated sometimes not sitting in the right posture?

Rinpoche: This does not mean that our posture should be imperfect. We should try our best, making sure our back is very straight, also not leaning to the right or left, or back or front. However, all humans are different and the main thing is to do the best we can.

Question: Why can't we have our palms facing upwards on our knees when we meditate?

Rinpoche: When you sit with your hands in that position, you are inviting energies and forces from outside (and hence distractions).

Question: I'm keen to sit in a full Lotus – how should I proceed?

Rinpoche: You can use various exercises to make your body more supple. However, the most important thing is to go gradually. If the postures do not come easily at the beginning, then only sit in them for a short time at the beginning in order not to strain the body. Otherwise the possibility of sitting in the Lotus posture will be impaired.

2. RELAXING

General Guidance

One of the essential aspects of 'Taming the Tiger' is learning to know when to relax and generally be able to be with yourself, whatever you are feeling. This kind of relaxed mind is a good basis for developing maturity and stability. In order to relax it is helpful to know oneself well. For example, some people are too loose whilst others are too uptight or tense. For someone too loose to give themselves too many breaks will water down the effects of these exercises and so be counter-productive. On the other hand for someone very uptight to be too severe on themselves again will create obstacles. Such people, if they knew themselves well, would give themselves breaks accordingly. Simple and clear self-knowledge will help us discover the middle way, beyond extremes. To do this we have to find out who we are beyond self-deception.

We can also develop a feeling for when something that we are doing is stirring us up or making an existing problem worse. In such situations, we can give ourselves a little break or spend more time relaxing. These exercises are to help us become stable and calm so it would be deeply ironical if we were to become uptight and tense doing them. However if we encounter disturbing circumstances for just a few days then that can be quite understandable since we may be touching on areas that were repressed or unseen before. This is quite natural. There will be reactions but the thing to realise is that they are not a big deal and to learn how to accept whatever comes up. That involves seeing the whole process and not becoming fixated on any one part of it.

Cultivating a non-reactive mind will itself help us to feel at ease. When a session goes badly, it is unwise to just jump up and switch on the TV or radio to try to distract oneself. There should be the ability to let all experience, inner and outer, come and go in an easy flow without being either too up or too down reacting according to how things are going. (For people who are easily distracted it is unwise to overdo the break – simply get up and stretch or something like that. Do not go out of the room or start a conversation half way through otherwise it will be very hard to get into the exercise again).

There seem to be two main problems when people try to relax. Some people cannot relax because there is a feeling, 'I have to be relaxed' and when the feeling of calmness does not come, then a feeling of panic arises. So when we try to do relaxation exercises, it is very important that we do not over-react – whatever happens. Even if we are unable to be calm, just simply accept whatever comes.

The other problem is that when a feeling of relaxation does arise one can get involved with it and consequently attached to it. Happiness and excitement can arise from this relaxation one day but when one comes to do the exercise the next day, one has expectations that a similar feeling should arise. If it does not, again there is a tendency to either panic or become very disappointed. You think – 'good feelings arose yesterday, then why not today?' There is a kind of warfare going on with oneself. This is itself an obstacle to relaxation. So the important thing is to have no expectations and to simply accept whatever happens.

The way to relax is to learn how to accept yourself. Let go of any expectations about, 'I'm doing this exercise – I should have this result or that result.' Instead cultivate the ability to know yourself and be with whatever you are thinking or feeling. Making friends with yourself without fighting yourself – that is the way to find relaxation very easily. To someone whose mind is really mature, they can be very happy wherever they are, whatever happens because they have learnt to accept themselves and whatever they experience.

Relaxing/Breathing

The relaxation exercises given here are based on breathing. One or the other of them should be done before beginning each session. In the first one, basing the breath on the count of five is a general guide-line, but it is important to adapt to the individual breathing pattern and to the immediate situation. As long as there is no strain, the in-breath can be a little deeper than usual, until a feeling of fullness arises. If one has much suffering or is in an emotional state, the whole cycle can be done a little faster. If one is feeling quite calm and relaxed, the whole cycle can be taken more slowly.

Wherever there is difficulty in relaxing when doing the breathing exercises, or any other exercise, it is good simply to lie down for a little while and let all thoughts and feelings come and go naturally. Then you can try the exercise again with less force.

The Exercises

1. Breathing/Relaxing

At first become aware of the stability of your body as it is resting on the ground. Feel your body as a whole and the environment around it. Then breathe in deeply to the count of five (or four or six, whatever comes naturally).

Hold the breath for the count of five.

Breathe out for the count of five – through the mouth as this gives a more complete release of tension. Do not hold after the out-breath, but continue naturally to the next in-breath.

With each out-breath visualise all tension flowing out, like emptying a pot of stale water, and let the mind go free.

Repeat at least three or four times.

2. Breathing/Relaxing

Alternatively, exhale through the mouth just very slightly longer than usual, pause for a moment...
Inhale through the nostrils just very slightly slower and deeper than usual, pause for a moment...
Exhale ... Repeat twenty-one times counting one exhalation plus one inhalation as one cycle of breath.

Either of these methods of relaxation should be practised for at least four days at the start of the series. Then they may be used before sessions or whenever tension arises in doing other exercises. They also may be helpful when experiencing tension in day-to-day situations.

Question: In certain circumstances, would you suggest that one version of the exercise might be preferable to the other, or is it simply a matter of personal choice?
Rinpoche: Some people may prefer one version; others may find the second version more agreeable to them. I think that's fine – whichever is easier to relate to.

Question: In the first version of the exercise specifically, should the breath be held with the throat open or closed?
Rinpoche: Whatever is natural, that would be better.

Question: Sometimes when I'm doing these breathing exercises I still feel tense, or even become more tense than before. Does that mean I'm breathing in the wrong way?
Rinpoche: Not necessarily. I don't think you need to worry too much about the breathing. Simply lie down and try to relax naturally; or it may be beneficial to go through the feeling exercise given in the next chapter.

Question: Rinpoche, as an asthma sufferer, I tend to experience fear associated with the breathing exercises. How can I overcome this?

Rinpoche: In that case I don't think it's essential to do the breathing exercises. Try simply to relax instead.

Question: If I'm interrupted by the telephone, for example, while doing the exercise, is it harmful to break off halfway and then come back afterwards and carry on where I left off?
Rinpoche: Well that's not necessarily a harmful thing, but if there are interruptions and distractions all the time then the value of the exercise will certainly be reduced.

3. General Relaxation Exercise

At first become aware of the stability of your body as it is resting on the ground. Feel your body as a whole and the environment around it. Now look into space, breathing out all the anxiety, tension or negative feelings. When you become calmer, simply watch all thoughts, feelings and external phenomena like a bystander at a parade. You are happy to watch the parade go by without jumping on every float! Be aware of, and recognise, what happens but you do not have to do anything else above that. Acknowledge all the thoughts or feelings but don't react to them or make any judgements about them. This is called mindfulness of each instant. Don't label thoughts as being positive or negative – simply recognise them and be aware.

The length of the exercise can be as long as you like. It can be done at a desk at work, or lying down on your back, anywhere.

Question: What is the most useful situation in which to do this exercise?
Rinpoche: Any situation – whatever is possible or appropriate.

3. Feeling

In this exercise we learn to come to terms with the most basic facts of our lives: what we actually feel. Relaxation is a beneficial side effect of looking into our experience at the level of bodily feeling. By applying the mind to something personal, yet often avoided, many fears and tensions may resolve themselves. The ability to perceive our feelings and sensations very accurately, accepting them all, pleasant and unpleasant, is a strong basis for facing things as they are in outer situations.

Many people tend to cultivate pleasant feelings, physical and emotional, and run away from negative ones. Or we may be obsessed with our pain and have difficulty in noticing and acknowledging that pain is not solid. Pain is always changing and is mixed together with neutral and positive aspects of experience. By repeating this exercise again and again we become familiar with the workings of impermanence at the most intimate level and are able to relax about it. Also the activity of paying attention is relaxing in itself.

The Exercise

1. Establishing the Situation

Sitting with a straight spine or lying on the back in a symmetrical position, we feel the body in contact with the seat or floor. Feel all points of contact, noticing where there is most pressure. Notice also that pressure may change slightly with the movement of breathing in and out. Once we have this overall situation of the body lying or sitting still (except for the subtle movement of breathing in and out in a natural way), we will examine the sensations in more detail.

2. Feeling the Sensations of the Body in More Detail

Beginning with the big toes on both feet, feel any sensations whatsoever in each of the toes. If there is no feeling, simply be aware of this and move on to the next pair of toes, noticing the right side and left side together.

Keeping the mind moving steadily, move up through the feet, noticing all the tiny differences of sensation – cold, warm, heavy, tingling, dull, sharp, throbbing, floating etc. – just noticing – not getting involved in telling stories about the feelings, but rather just feeling them.

We continue moving the mind up the legs to the hips. Then starting with the fingers, move the attention up the hands and arms to the shoulders. Then we shift the attention back down to the base of the spine and very gradually move upwards, vertebra by vertebra, simply observing the sensations at each level; both in the spine itself and in the rest of the torso. Notice all the many sensations related to various internal organs and the movement of the breath. As far as possible, simply feel without labelling or analysing.

When you reach the neck, continue up the neck and the throat, feeling the outside and inside, and continue on up into the mouth. Travel with awareness through the various parts of the face and head, inside and outside, letting the attention come to rest at the very top of the head in the centre.

Then reverse the flow of attention but let the mind move quite a bit more quickly. Imagine the body hollow and filled with water. The plug is pulled at your feet and the water drains out – follow the line where the water would be from top to bottom, feeling the fields of sensation at each level rather than taking the body part by part. When you reach your toes again, bring your attention to the natural movement of the breath in the body as a whole; simply watch the movement of the breath, in a relaxed unfocused way for the rest of the session. At the end of the session, stretch the body very completely.

It is important that after each sequence of moving attention from the feet to the head, the flow is reversed moving from the head to the feet. Some people find it more comfortable and relaxing always to move the attention from head to feet.

Do this for approximately 1 hour for one week and return to it when necessary for relaxation.

Question: What should one do if very painful sensations arise during the feeling exercise and it's impossible to ignore them and carry on?
Rinpoche: In the first place it might be helpful to repeat the relaxation exercises, rather than trying to force the practice; but if these painful sensations recur over a period of months then it may be necessary to stay with the sensations and try to face them.

Question: When you say 'repeat the relaxation exercises', do you mean repeat one of the breathing relaxation exercises?
Rinpoche: I think perhaps just lie down and let the sensations subside – try not to worry about anything.

Question: Sometimes during this exercise my attention refuses to move through a certain part of the body; it seems to get stuck somewhere or other. What can I do then?
Rinpoche: Maybe you're trying to move something too heavy or solid, or you're pushing too hard. Sometimes a screw won't go through the hole because it's too big for the hole. Then you need one a little smaller; you need to proceed more lightly.

Question: When strong emotions or memories keep recurring, inspired by the sensations I'm feeling, is it useful to examine and analyse these experiences, or should I try to concentrate on the physical sensations themselves?

Rinpoche: Just try to go along with the sensations and don't take too much notice of whatever arises from them.

Question: While doing this exercise I started to feel sensations that I've never felt at any other time. Is this just my imagination at work?

Rinpoche: Not necessarily. It could be that the sensations were there all along, but that you're only now becoming aware of them – you're beginning to see more clearly. Slowing down the mind in this exercise may bring awareness of things that you did not notice before. That is fine. However, one should simply feel and not add on to the feeling experienced. Many therapies make people read too much into into every little feeling in the body implying that they have some special psychological meaning. This can make people more and more sensitive and so less and less able to face whatever comes up. This is not the purpose of this exercise. Instead one is simply training the mind to accept whatever arises without analysing or becoming involved with the emotions.

Question: What happens if you do this exercise and you feel nothing at all in your body.

Rinpoche: There is always something. Start with sensations that you cannot miss like the expanding of your waistband. Be satisfied with the obvious, what you can feel rather than worrying about what you cannot. Use this as a basis to go on from there to gradually feel more and more. It is important not to worry about feeling nothing. It is unnecessary to feel guilty or unhappy about how little you feel during the exercise. Just simply carry on with it.

4. The Golden Light of Universal Compassion

With this exercise we cultivate the attitude of being open to others and learning how to serve them. Open up to all of your thoughts, feelings, sensations, with the awareness that your natural experience is the raw material for your positive development. This refers not only to good experience. Even very negative thoughts or emotions can become the basis of compassion. For example, if someone has a lot of anger, that person will go on having negative feelings to other angry people until their own anger is acknowledged. Once they do recognise their own anger and its harmful consequences within: then there arises naturally a feeling of compassion to others who suffer from anger because they realise how dreadful it is to be in that state. Even anger can be a source of compassion.

So, in this exercise we are given the chance, in the moment, to acknowledge our own experience and then to make that experience useful and valuable to others through the process of transformation.

First of all, it is necessary to make contact with whatever you are experiencing (whether it be physical, emotional, intellectual – whatever). Allow yourself to become aware of what your mood is, what your emotions are, then notice what thoughts are coming in and out of your mind. Try not to block anything but to have confidence that you are going to work with whatever arises. As thoughts and feelings arise let them flow out to benefit all beings. Cultivate the feeling, 'from now on I am working for the good of everyone'. This exercise is also useful for relaxation, because no thoughts or feelings, no matter how destructive or disturbing, need to be suppressed. All are equally and immediately valuable in the development of compassion. So this is an excellent exercise for letting go of repressed and bottled-up feelings.

The Exercise

Take at least five minutes 'establishing the situation'. Find yourself a comfortable sitting position with your spine upright or make yourself comfortable lying down. Feel the space around you, where you are and become aware of the sensations of the body as it is resting on the ground. Be aware of the breath as it comes in and out of the body – do relaxation breathing exercises if necessary and then start the exercise.

Resolve that whatever arises, whether it be positive, negative, or neutral – that you will accept it all as being useful as the raw material for the development of compassion. Look at whatever is going on within you, all the three kinds of experience – physical, emotional and mental. Visualise a completely open space. In the centre of the space you see a gate or doorway that opens outwards. Now focus on the outbreath. Whatever thoughts, feelings, sensations arise – you breathe them out through the gate with the confidence that they are being transformed into universal compassion in the form of golden light which passes through the gate to all who live. Feel that this golden light of compassion is equally available to everyone everywhere, fulfilling all of their needs and wishes.

Gradually feel that the whole of space is filled with this golden light and that absolutely no-one is excluded from the influence of universal compassion and that, in fact, in the end, it comes back to you. Feel that you also are included in the field of compassion and that whatever you are needing or wanting comes to you the same as to all the others.

This meditation should be done twenty minutes a day for two weeks. However, if at any stage during the sequence of meditations following you become tense, you may return to this practice for a day or so before continuing with the series.

Question: After you breathe out through the gate, does the gate remain open, or does it close again on each in-breath?
Rinpoche: The gate remains open; but if you see it opening on the out-breath and closing on the in-breath, that is alright too.

Question: If one focuses solely on the out-breath, do the thoughts and feelings continue to flow through the gate even on the in-breath?
Rinpoche: Yes, they do. (Whether you focus on them or not.)

Question: Rather than visualising the gate in front of me, in space, is it alright to think of myself as the gate?
Rinpoche: There shouldn't be any harm in that.

Question: And if one extends the focus to where the light goes, visualising those who are suffering actually receiving what they need, is that alright, too?
Rinpoche: No reason why not. You can either send the light to all those, in general, who are in suffering; or to a particular person or persons.

Question: Could this exercise be used to work on difficult personal relationships? For example, if someone treats me as if I'm always in the wrong, would it be useful to imagine all my anger and resentment passing through the gate and changing into the golden light of compassion so that they might feel better and stop blaming me?
Rinpoche: That could be beneficial, yes.

Question: What if I am not in the mood for benefitting others when I am doing this exercise? Should I do another exercise or visualise the golden light without it going out to others?
Rinpoche: I don't think it ever happens that you don't want to do anyone any good. Even if you don't want to benefit everyone, there must be at least one or two people you wish to be happy. So

you can start out with the golden light going out to someone you wish to benefit and try to develop that same feeling for everyone.

Question: Are the feelings visualised in certain shapes and forms, like the movie of the mind or as smoke, before they reach the gate? Or is it purely a matter of feeling?
Rinpoche: I don't think you will actually see the smoke – it's really just a matter of feeling.

5. Rainbow

In previous exercises we have used inner objects – the breath, bodily sensations, and a visualisation generating compassion for working with the mind. In the rainbow exercise we will look at outer objects with a focused mind, attempting to see their true nature.

There are different categories of objects we might choose from:
a) objects which have a material value (e.g. a gemstone).
b) objects which have no cash value and do not belong to us (e.g. a pebble or a blade of grass).
c) objects belonging to us, whether of material worth or not; anything we think of as ours or mine.

The value of this exercise is threefold:
1) to look at the mind's tendency to cling to objects and the way clinging interferes with seeing things as they are.
2) to contemplate the non-solid and impermanent nature of all things – even those which appear solid. (This view accords with the understandings of contemporary science.)
3) to overcome the fear, which many people have, that they cannot visualise. Here the object is always available before our eyes, so there is no need to strain. In this way we learn naturally how to build up a visualisation and how to let go of it again.

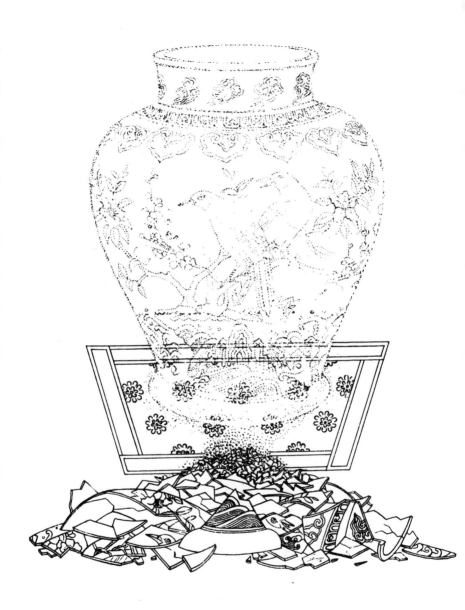

The Exercise

Take at least five minutes 'establishing the situation'. Find yourself a comfortable sitting position with your spine upright. Feel the space around you where you are and become aware of the sensations of the body as it is resting on the ground. Be aware of the breath as it comes in and out of the body – do relaxation breathing exercises if necessary and then start the exercise.

The aim is to take an object and change it into a rainbow in your mind. First of all, select something belonging to you but of no great value. Place it in front of you so that you can see the whole thing. Think of its value and reflect on this. With the eyes still open, next visualise another one just like it before you in space. Now imagine you are breaking it into pieces. Gradually it is broken into smaller and smaller pieces which you systematically destroy. Finally, think of the tiniest pieces being pounded down to dust. The particles are so small they are almost invisible. Put the particles together in a heap so that not a speck of dust is lost. Then ask: 'Where is the object?"

Now reflect: 'When I began there was an object, a name and a value. Now where is the object, the name, or the value?'

Next, in your mind, turn the dust into a rainbow. It can be a rainbow of one colour or of many colours. From this rainbow of dust, recreate the object as a rainbow-object. It is back to being just the same as the original object, but you can see it has no solidity – it is a rainbow.

Reflect that now it has no material worth.

Finally melt the rainbow object into the original object before you. Note how your appreciation of it, your sense of its value, may have changed.

While doing this exercise the eyes should remain open looking into near space but with the object still peripherally visible so there is no need to doubt one's ability to visualise it.

During the meditation, if you begin to feel tired or tense, you should take short breaks (like taking a minute or two to rest the body, especially the eyes and the mind) or, if it is appropriate, do one of the relaxing meditations given earlier. For people who are

easily distracted it is unwise to overdo the break – simply get up
and stretch or something like that. Do not go out of the room or
start a conversation half way through otherwise it will be very
hard to get into the exercise again.

Each time you do the exercise, use a different object. Begin
with an object which has relatively little value for you and work
up to something of greater value. Also select a variety of types of
objects. For example, you could focus on a painting in your mind,
gradually strip it down, remove the paint, break down the paint,
shred the canvas and splinter the frame. If you choose a tapestry,
dismantle and break down the threads into their components.

Do this meditation for one hour each day for a week.

*Question: If it's easier to see the imagined object and the process
of breaking it down with the eyes closed, is this as effective as
keeping them open?*
Rinpoche: If you find that the exercise is more effective with the
eyes closed, that's fine; but in general it's probably better to keep
them open as much as you can.

*Question: I've found that this exercise increases my appreciation
of the original object in regard to its nature and what it's made up
of. Is this part of the purpose of the exercise?*
Rinpoche: Yes! When you see that everything is in essence no
more substantial than a rainbow, then you will have more appreciation of its true nature. You'll be able to use it properly.

*Question: What about when you start to prefer the rainbow, when
you enjoy destroying the object with a form? Isn't this the wrong
way of looking at it?*
Rinpoche: Not wrong, necessarily, for the time being at any rate.
Of course it wouldn't do to get carried away – there has to be a
limit. When you say 'destroying' it gives the idea of force – yet
'destroying' and 'understanding' are two different things. What
we are trying to do is understand the nature of the object, how it
was created. An example would be a work of art. When you do

the exercise, you remove all the red, yellow etc. Each time you remove the colour in your mind, you see what is happening. Then you take away all the threads of the canvas, seeing how it is created. It is like you had a video of how the painting was created – you realise that it is not something solid. Each colour or thread is not a cause of attachment or suffering. However you must remember that it is not like getting a sharp knife and destroying the canvas with anger.

Question: When I do this exercise with my eyes open and the object in front of me, the object becomes distracting and the exercise becomes very difficult. Can you do the rainbow exercise without anything in front of you at all?
Rinpoche: Yes. You could look at the object first and then visualise the object or you can visualise the object first and then go through all the stages. It is also alright to sometimes just visualise the object there in front of you.

Question: Should we visualise with our eyes closed or open?
Rinpoche: Generally I encourage people to meditate, and visualise, with their eyes open. If people train from the beginning to keep their eyes shut when they are doing their practice, later on it will be very hard for them to break that habit. However, if you find it impossible for any reason to keep them open, then from time to time it is possible to close them. In the beginning especially, it may be alright to visualise with your eyes closed using the object from time to time as a reference point. However, in the long run, it is very valuable to be able to visualise with your eyes open – that way you are gradually developing the mind in such a way that the awareness of visual phenomena is not a distraction. This applies to everything else as well as visualisation. You tame your mind so that whether your eyes are open or closed, you will remain undistracted wherever you are. That way you have choice of how you think and feel and it is not conditioned by whatever it is that you are seeing. It is necessary to learn to meditate in the midst of distractions instead of always trying to shut them out.
    (Many people teach meditation techniques where the eyes are

supposed to be closed. For the first month or so this may be OK but after one year the practitioners can become very tense. This does not happen the same way for those who keep their eyes open. It is also very hard for someone to change after keeping their eyes closed for the first few years; there could even be a feeling of panic when they try to change. So, in the beginning, it is best to train in the right way. Of course, there's no harm from time to time closing the eyes in the way of relaxation.)

Question: One of the objects I'm using for this exercise was given to me by my mother and I feel great resistance to 'smashing' this in my mind. How do I deal with this?
Rinpoche: To begin with, the idea is not to be 'smashing' anything. Things may become complicated if you see the exercise that way. If there is resistance to dealing with this kind of object, then that can be very meaningful and all the more valuable to go through it. However the wise thing to do in the beginning is to go forward gradually. Everything that we experience we either like, dislike or feel neutral about. Sometimes we feel we like something very much and then, a few days later, we do not like it any more. So if you have this particular preference thinking, 'I don't want to dissolve this' then at another time that feeling could change radically. One of the important things to discover from this exercise is how we project values onto objects. Every object is created from tiny atoms – although its appearance is quite solid, its nature is not. The object itself can be stolen or broken. If at that time we do the rainbow exercise, you can learn to see beyond appearances. You are able to keep the preciousness of what your mother has given to you whether the object is there or not. By understanding the rainbow exercise properly you can appreciate it fully. If you do not, then there is much suffering if the object changes or is broken. At this time the object will become more rather than less valuable since you understand its impermanent non-solid nature.

Question: I feel a lot of anger or resistance to dissolving precious objects, how do I deal with that?

Rinpoche: It is useful not to force anything in the beginning, so start with an object you feel comfortable about dissolving. Then, when you feel satisfied with this, you can then go on from there to more difficult objects.

Question: If I have something like a pound note or a great work of literature, the feeling comes it is not mine to destroy. How do I deal with that?
Rinpoche: The idea of the 'Rainbow Exercise' is not to destroy. The idea of the dissolving is to try to understand that the pound note or the book are only printed on paper – a process. They are not something solid or really belonging to anyone. So the exercise is to try to understand this – not to destroy but appreciate the true nature of the object.

Question: This exercise stirs up a lot of attachment – I find myself not wanting to let go of some things. Could you please say something on this?
Rinpoche: I think all of our emotions or feelings, whether they are positive or negative, they all have to change. They are changing all the time anyway just like the objects themselves. We have to learn to accept this impermanence – that way we will have less attachment to what we are doing. Generally, in order to mature our minds, we have to let go of strong attachments.

Question: I find it very difficult to visualise. What shall I do?
Rinpoche: Many people say they cannot visualise but this is not true. Everyone has the seed of visualisation in their minds. It is a mental experience that is powerful, vivid and clear. If someone is in love and their loved one is with someone else, then they can visualise every detail, a whole sequence of events. Indeed, the whole 'picture' appears effortlessly! In that situation you cannot stop – you are out of control. But when we visualise in these exercises we must retain control. Since our minds visualise anyway – why not turn this capacity into something positive and useful? It can be very useful for healing the mind and deepening our

understanding.

Some people say they cannot visualise – that it is too difficult but it is a question of how much effort you are prepared to put into it. It will help if you give the process your whole heart.

Question: Could the word 'imagine' cover what you mean by the word 'visualise'?
Rinpoche: Yes. It is a very similar meaning – if you are hungry, you imagine good food or visualise good food. It is very much the same thing.

6. The Mirror

The purpose of the next exercise is to help us to become aware of and to understand the process of projection. Projection here refers to the mind's tendency to see things outside according to inner feelings and understandings. We all know that if we are in an especially unhappy mood then there seems to be an endless supply of things we can focus on outside which justify and increase our unhappiness. Inasmuch as we are aware of this process of projection, and take responsibility for it, we are on the way to maturing the mind.

However, it is our lack of awareness of the process of projection which causes danger and difficulty. We see faults in family members and associates, but deny their existence in ourselves. We fail to see that the qualities we most wish to deny in ourselves are the ones we will be most likely to project on to others, and to which we will react in a very emotional way. We may also project our own positive potential and qualities on to others, not wishing to take responsibility for cultivating, nurturing and owning these in ourselves, preferring to see others as 'good' and ourselves as hopeless and 'bad'.

The exercise 'The Mirror' teaches us that we can work with our feelings – being aware of projecting them. In Phase 1 we can see and let go of the ones which do not help, whilst keeping and developing the ones that do. In Phase 2 of 'The Mirror', we see how our projections come back to us, affecting the whole of experience until the time that we can see them for what they are. It is important that this exercise should be done in short sessions only – about fifteen or twenty minutes once or twice a day. At least five or ten minutes of relaxation should precede and follow each session.

The Exercise

Take at least five minutes 'establishing the situation'. Find yourself a comfortable sitting position with your spine upright. Feel the space around you, where you are and become aware of the sensations of the body as it is resting on the ground. Be aware of the breath as it comes in and out of the body – do relaxation breathing exercises if necessary and then start the exercise.

Phase 1

Sit in front of a mirror, preferably one which allows you to see your whole body. First think to yourself that the mirror is a piece of glass holding an image, a reflection which is only 'there' by virtue of what you see in it.

Sit for about ten minutes with eyes closed or looking down, just relaxing, being aware of sensations, thoughts and emotions. Make a point of noticing negative and positive in a balanced way. Then, after a few minutes, when the mind begins to settle naturally, look at your reflection. First look at yourself in the mirror, noticing whatever thoughts and feelings come up. Then, focusing on the outbreath only, breathe all thoughts, feelings and emotions into your reflection in the mirror. Feel that you are gradually emptying yourself, letting go of the feelings, moving them into the mirror. Feel that you are moving your whole self into the mirror. Allow a sense of non-solidity, transparency to arise, a sense of space between you and your thoughts.

After fifteen or twenty minutes, bring back into yourself all the positive qualities you choose, leaving the negative, whatever you feel you can do without, in the mirror.

Be aware that it was your own projections which created all you see in the mirror. Be aware that it is by choice and understanding you can take back into yourself all the pure and positive qualities you have recognised.

After fifteen or twenty minutes of working with your projections in the mirror, take five or ten minutes simply to relax the mind, letting thoughts come and go with an easy flow. Continue this first phase for at least one week or until it becomes quite easy to project feelings into the mirror and you feel some confidence in a less solid way of experiencing. Until this confidence comes, it is better not to proceed to Phase 2 of the exercise.

Phase 2

Begin in the same way as Phase 1 – simply sitting, allowing the mind to settle. Then, when you look at your reflection, practise exchanging who you feel yourself to be with the person you see in the mirror. Whatever you feel in yourself, breathe this with each outbreath into the person you see there. Whoever you see in the mirror, bring all the thoughts and feelings of that person into yourself with each in-breath. Continue exchanging in this way, remaining as mindful as possible that all you are experiencing is your own projection. It is important not to try to analyse but simply to do the exercise, staying within the time limit and relaxing at the end.

'The Mirror' is very important in opening us to the true basis of our experience of ourselves and others. Many of the exercises which follow involve exchanging with projected images of friends, family members, enemies, etc. These exercises are not truly valid until we understand deeply and properly what we mean by 'our own projections'. Thus 'The Mirror' exercises should not be skipped over by those wishing to continue the course.

If you have major obstacles and are unable to complete 'The Mirror' due to strong fear or other intense reactions, then it is possible to go on to do 'Awakening our Potential' then to 'Expanding and Contracting' and then to 'The Rainbow Sphere'. At another stage you may find you are ready to try 'The Mirror' again, and will then be able to progress through each of the other exercises involving projection.

Time:

Phase 1: 15-20 min. once or twice daily, minimum one week.
Phase 2: 15-20 min. daily for three or four weeks.

Question: Rinpoche. While doing the first phase of the exercise, I've been able to transfer a lot of painful feelings from my body into the mirror, and this has been a great relief. But isn't this just some kind of trick?
Rinpoche: In a sense every exercise could be called a trick, but the exercises do provide the opportunity and means for training the mind. Whereas the exercise can't really take away one's pain and suffering – it has no ultimate benefit in this respect – still there can be benefit in the short term.

Question: I was wondering if the mirror exercises could be regarded as a lesson in impermanence. I mean could I think of it in that way? Or should I just stick to moving the feelings from myself to the mirror and back?
Rinpoche: You may look at the reflection and see it as transparent and impermanent and extend that to everything you see. That's good, it's a useful example. Or you may simply use it temporarily to release tension, to bring your inner problems to the surface. That's also useful. It's up to you how to use it.

Question: If I leave all my negative and bad experiences in the mirror, isn't that a bit untidy? I mean shouldn't I mentally clean the mirror before anyone else uses it?
Rinpoche: No, I don't think that's necessary. The mirror doesn't feel pain and suffering, or store it up. The idea is to let some of one's pain and suffering out, to empty oneself a little. It's like a cup of tea – when it's too full you can't hold it without spilling some, you have to pour some away. Similarly with one's feelings – you have to empty yourself a little. The mirror is useful for that.

Question: During the second phase of the exercise, what I saw in the mirror made me very unhappy. Then, when I took it into myself, I felt worse still. The only thing that helped was to remind myself that neither my feelings nor the reflection was solid at all. Was this the right way to see it, a valid way of solving the problem?

Rinpoche: Yes. If you look in a mirror, it's most important to realise that what you see is not at all solid. So whether joyful or depressing feelings arise during the exercise, you don't take either too seriously. Since neither is solid, you don't put too much value on such feelings.

Question: What if strange visual effects should occur when I look in the mirror?

Rinpoche: Seeing yourself in strange distorted ways is not the purpose of this exercise. After a certain time, which may differ from person to person, certain visual distortions may arise – if this happens, simply rest the eyes, relax, and begin again. They are physical phenomena due to eyestrain. Don't worry about them. The purpose of the exercise is to see yourself more clearly as you really are – not to get involved in strange visual effects. If they persist, you could try doing shorter sessions.

Question: What if you find that you can understand projection intellectually but you cannot apply it to yourself?

Rinpoche: Quite simply you just need to go ahead and apply it to yourself, whichever way you can.

7. Friend

The object of this exercise is to understand attachment. We have such a powerful attachment to some people or objects that it is not easy to separate ourselves from them. The exercise also gives us a chance to gain understanding of our friends based on all we know of them, rather than what we want from them. By exchanging, which includes giving what we know of ourselves, we may also be able to increase our openness in what we are willing and able to express and give to others who are close to us. A positive motivation is crucial here as with all of the other exercises. The exchange helps us learn to understand ourselves and our friends better and thus be able to feel and act with compassion. Otherwise we may endlessly repeat negative behaviour based on our own selfish and one-sided point of view.

The Exercise

Take at least five minutes 'establishing the situation'. Find yourself a comfortable sitting position with your spine upright. Feel the space around you, where you are and become aware of the sensations of the body as it is resting on the ground. Be aware of the breath as it comes in and out of the body – do relaxation breathing exercises if necessary and then start the exercise.

1. First session – Projecting

Think of a person you are attached to – someone you very much want to be with. It can be anyone you feel very close to – parent, wife, husband, boy-friend, girl-friend, lover, child or any other close friend. See this person in front of you, but most important, feel that they are really there. Allow yourself enough time, thinking and projecting in this way, for the image and sense of the presence of the person to develop very clearly in front of you.

Do this for about ten or fifteen minutes and then take a short break.

2. Second session – Exchanging

As you breathe in, imagine that you are breathing your friend who sits before you, into yourself. As you breathe out, you breathe yourself into your friend. Your friend's outer form and your outer form remain the same, but gradually the contents are exchanged. All your thoughts, feelings, sensations and desires flow, bit by bit, with the out-breath, into your friend, and his or hers are drawn into you with the in-breath. It is not necessary to exchange with every single breath. Try to keep the flow back and forth as natural and as easy as possible – not censoring or structuring, but giving and receiving whatever comes up. Continue this for half an hour. At the end of the session you may stay with the feeling of being your friend or come back to your own feelings – whichever you choose. However, in either case, keep the understanding of the friend within you.

Do this meditation once a day for forty-five minutes. Continue for three or four weeks. As you progress, use different friends as the focus of your meditation.

Question: What if the person I'm thinking of won't stay sitting still but is always roaming around, appearing and disappearing?
Rinpoche: That's okay. They don't have to sit. You're the one who is sitting.

Question: Most of the time I feel a complete block with this exercise, which seems to be based on fear against taking in or giving out at all at this level. The feeling of separation is very strong. What should I do?
Rinpoche: In that case, you spend a longer time with 'The Mirror' in order to break down the sense of solidity. This feeling of solidity is what's creating the difficulties for you, especially the difficulty to exchange. You have this fear, so do more mirror practice until the fear of non-solidity is overcome.

Question: Couldn't it be a bit presumptuous or even dangerous to take on the whole experience of another person like this?
Rinpoche: No, there won't be any danger. You would have to be fairly advanced for any problem to arise. Since you are practising with the right motivation, when that danger comes, you will be out of it.

Question: If I already feel very close and very involved with somebody, very attached, won't the process of mentally getting so close to them just increase the attachment.
Rinpoche: No. I think that 'The Mirror' will solve that problem too.

Question: What if when doing the exercise I get a very strong physical and emotional experience of the other person's problems, the other person's pain, which I didn't even know about before and this experience is very overwhelming because I don't know what I can do to help?
Rinpoche: I can't see that will happen. Most of what you feel is your own created pain, rather than that you are able to feel someone else's suffering. However, even if it is more than imagination, the right attitude is to have very much compassion for the other person. You fully realize what is painful, what they're going through and make the wish, 'May I be able to help.'

Question: How long should we stay with one friend before going on to the next, and is it better to start with friendships which are

simpler and have less attachment?
Rinpoche: You can stay with one friend as long as is necessary.
It's good to work both with very close ones and not so close ones.

8. Awakening Our Potential

Here, the sphere of golden light is used as the symbol of the awakened state of mind: total awareness and perfect wisdom blended with universal compassion. For anyone who has any objection or problem with visualising a sphere of pure golden light, the Buddha, Christ or a great religious teacher may be visualised to express the same qualities: awakeness and compassion, perfect purity of mind. If one has faith and conviction in the Buddha or Christ, then it will be very effective. The main thing to remember is that the qualities of wisdom and compassion are the important thing and that the form one can relate to most easily and most effectively is the one to be used.

The Exercise

1. Foundation

Take at least five minutes 'establishing the situation'. Find yourself a comfortable sitting position with your spine upright. Feel the space around you, where you are and become aware of the sensations in your whole body as it is resting on the ground. Be aware of the breath as it comes in and out of the body. If your breath is restricted, then go through one of the relaxation breathing exercises given at the beginning of the second section. Then let yourself be aware of the outbreath, letting go of tension or obstacles and then, when you feel at ease, start the exercise.

Making certain that your posture is upright, think of a yellow lotus, also upright, at the centre of your body.

Think now of a hollow tube which begins at the crown of your head (the point where the hair forms a circle). The top of this tube is like a wide funnel – very open. The tube comes down through your body and joins onto the lotus, entering into its heart. The tube has no particular colour.

2. Invitation

Visualise a beautiful sphere of golden light of any size resting just above the opening of the funnel. Feel and see your body becoming less and less solid, more and more open and transparent.

3. Entry

Bring the beautiful transparent form of the sphere down through the funnel into the centre of your body to the heart of the lotus. Do not think of the golden light form or your body as solid at all.

Do this meditation for forty-five minutes, then take a break.

4. Relax

Do the relaxation meditation. This can be done either sitting up or lying down but the most important thing is to take the time to let go. Since this is a long relaxation session, it is important to be comfortable enough i.e. if you are lying down make sure that you are warm and comfortable enough with a small cushion or pillow underneath your head. Make sure however that you are not too warm and inclined to fall asleep! If you are relaxing sitting down, be at ease and not in a forced position – here the back does not have to be dead straight.

Having established the situation, now allow the mind to rest and let thoughts, feelings and ideas come and go with an easy flow. Reflect that the essence of awakeness and compassion is now within me and everything around me. There are no solid body parts or organs, no pain or tension. All is allowed to dissolve into tranquillity and a peaceful state of mind.

Do this relaxation for about one hour. Each session lasts for about one hour and forty-five minutes and should be continued daily for one week.

Question: When you refer to the centre of the body, where is that precisely?
Rinpoche: This is normally the heart region, but that's not the only possibility. It depends where you feel the centre of your own body lies.

Question: If I can't actually see the form of the golden sphere in my mind, is it enough to feel that it is there?
Rinpoche: Yes, the aim is to locate the mind's essential goodness – the precise form of that quality is secondary.

Question: Rinpoche, sometimes, instead of a golden light, other colours appear. Should I keep trying for the golden colour?
Rinpoche: I think so. Some kind of golden colour would be the best.

Question: Can you suggest how this might more easily be achieved?
Rinpoche: Examine a piece of golden material. If, when you're looking at the material it becomes a very solid colour, then try looking at the golden colour reflected in a mirror. In this way, you may get some idea of the transparency of the colour.

Question: During the relaxation phase at the end of the exercise, often my mind isn't peaceful at all, lots of emotions arise. What

can I do about that?
Rinpoche: Try to find whatever tranquillity you can and let the emotions dissolve into that, along with your thoughts and ideas. Even if you're only a little peaceful, only one percent peaceful, this part of the exercise can still be accomplished.

Question: If there isn't time to spend the suggested one and three quarter hours on this exercise, is it still important to do the relaxation every time at the end?
Rinpoche: Yes, it is. However much time you have available, try to keep to the same proportions for each phase of the exercise.

Question: Why are there all the different timings for the exercises? Specifically, is one and three quarter hours necessary for 'Awakening Our Potential'?
Rinpoche: Some exercises should be longer than others. When dealing with something more profound, like this exercise, then it is necessary to spend the extra time. 'Awakening Our Potential' is the most essential exercise – it is a very effective means for understanding the true nature of the self.

Progress So Far

Before going ahead with the next exercise, let us review the value and progress of the preceding ones. All of the exercises are designed to follow one another. You may not gain understanding of them immediately, but if you keep practising, understanding will arise out of your efforts.

What we are dealing with here are our everyday situations. We are not trying to create something apart from them, or trying to bring anything new into effect. We have problems in our lives which we have created ourselves. But, for this very reason, because we have created them, we have the key to freeing ourselves from them.

We began with relaxing, feeling, and openness exercises, followed by the rainbow meditation – dissolving material objects into a less solid form. Afterwards we did the exercises with the mirror, and exchanging with a friend. The 'Rainbow', 'Friend' and 'Awakening our Potential' exercises showed that we can visualise; the only question is one of depth. To develop visualisation, we can use close attachment to a friend, lover, etc. as a starting point and then try to bring the image of the golden sphere to the same level of clarity. The process depends upon the degree to which we become involved with the person or projection. For example, when we fall in love or become very involved with a person, images of that person may arise very powerfully and spontaneously.

Everyone can visualise, but results depend on the time we are willing to spend and the right sort of effort. Inability to visualise is likely to come from trying too hard and in a tense way. Whereas if we enjoy the practice, and have full confidence in its potential benefit, then visualisation will begin to come easily and naturally.

If you can only see a friend or enemy when you are trying to visualise the golden sphere, don't worry about it. It means that you have to work to understand that all beings have the essence of compassion and awakeness within them. The only thing that obscures this is the division of people into 'enemies' and 'friends', and the tendency to see the negative in people rather than seeing their positive aspects. Although everybody has the essence of awakened mind within them, we have to practise and visualise in order to understand this.

9. Bringing that Potential to Life

The previous exercise involved visualising the sphere of golden light having all the qualities of wisdom and compassion, which we have not yet realised, within our bodies. In studying anatomy, we use models which are projected images of our organs, bones, etc. We do not have to tear our organs out to study them. It is the same with the sphere of golden light within – it is there whether we have forgotten it, or know how to see it, or not. Thus we begin by projecting an image outside in order to gain an understanding of what exists inside.

The Exercise

Take at least five minutes 'establishing the situation'. Find yourself a comfortable sitting position with your spine upright. Feel the space around you, where you are and become aware of the sensations of the body as it is resting on the ground. Be aware of the breath as it comes in and out of the body – do relaxation breathing exercises if necessary and then start the exercise.

The aim of this exercise is to bring the qualities of wisdom and compassion within to life. Since the previous exercise established the image of the golden light sphere (or a Buddha or a great religious teacher), in the heart of the inner lotus, it is unnecessary to go through the full process of creating and bringing it down. Begin simply by thinking of the sphere at the centre of your body. Focus on it, remembering that your body and that of the sphere are in a transparent, or rainbow form without opacity or weight. If you keep to the image of the rainbow body, the problems of shape, the direction that you are facing and so on, will not arise. We are not dealing with solid bodies which have to be organised in rigid ways.

1. Seeing the Friend in a Pure Way

The golden sphere of light, with all the qualities of kindness and understanding, is on a lotus at the centre of your body. As you breathe out, a sphere of golden light comes out of your body along with your breath, but the original sphere of light remains on the lotus. Allow an easy flow with about one sphere per breath, but don't try to stick rigidly to this.

See one friend from the earlier exercise sitting in front of you. As the golden light form leaves your body, allow this transparent form to dissolve into your friend so that the two are completely mixed and have the one compassionate and purely awakened essence. We saw how attachment led to knowing and understanding the friend. This same closeness now enables you to know and understand the sphere of golden light that is mixed with the friend. Gradually you will come to see your friend in his or her essential nature of wisdom and understanding.

2. Seeing Oneself in a Pure Way

Now you will also become the form of wisdom and compassion. Think to yourself, 'I am the embodiment of Awakeness and Compassion' or 'I am Buddha'. Now both you and your friend are in your rainbow bodies and bear no trace of your former identities. As sphere facing sphere (or Buddha facing Buddha) there is no question of 'me' or 'my friend'.

3. Resting in Positive Pride

If you wish, you can add a further stage to this meditation: developing a sense of innate dignity or 'positive pride'. This is not the pride of, 'I have so many wonderful qualities and am a very spiritual person.' It is something different. It is profound respect which comes from realising that all beings, including myself, are essentially pure. This is the opposite of selfish pride, because it brings a feeling of closeness to others and happiness to all. In fact it is a powerful and effective antidote to the kind of pride which makes us feel separate from, and better than, other people. So, while you see yourself and your friend as awakened beings, kind and compassionate, you feel the innate dignity of this reality and take pride in that. Remain in this certainty for a while.

If you become restless during the meditation, stop and do the relaxing breathing and then begin again. Do not force yourself to go on and do long sessions if there is a lot of restlessness. It is better to do a number of short sessions with breaks. Sessions can be as short as five minutes. The principle is to go according to your own limits.

Do this exercise once a day for one hour and fifteen minutes. Continue for four weeks.

Afterword

In this exercise we became aware of ourselves and our friends as essentially pure, the embodiment of wisdom and compassion, represented as spheres of golden light or Buddha. This enabled us to gain an important understanding: when we see ourselves and our friends as ordinary people, we have desire and attachment which give rise to clinging, delusion and hatred. But if we are both spheres of golden light, how can there be attachment? Grasping love becomes respect. Out of this we are able to develop the attitude of helping all people. Our problem is 'I' and 'my friend'. This gives rise to expectations and all of the negative consequences that follow from them. If we see all beings as essentially pure, their actions become essentially pure too and we can see them with a mind free of expectation, judgement or other negativity. We need to do this exercise over and over so that gradually our mind will realise its true state.

Question: Is it better to focus on a different person every day, and could this be an enemy instead of a friend?
Rinpoche: If you're trying to deal with one particular problem or obstacle then you may repeatedly use the person who embodies that obstacle until it has been overcome; but if the aim is simply to understand the true nature of kindness and understanding within everybody, then you can use a different person every day.

Question: Why is pride regarded as such a bad thing, when it helps people in society to maintain high standards for themselves, whilst setting the example for others to do the same?
Rinpoche: I think if you are a very proud person, in the beginning it is good to work with that pride by changing it into the positive pride described in the exercise. But in the long run pride is not useful because there is so much ego. For example, pride in the family – thinking 'I have such a nice family' – there is nothing wrong with that except what it is going to lead to next. Clinging to this idea of a nice family will produce problems.

Question: What if the friend I am using turns into someone else in the middle of the session? Should I go along with it or try to get back to the original subject?
Rinpoche: In the beginning you could try to go back to the original subject, to establish some measure of control of the visualisation; but beyond a certain level of development this isn't so necessary.

Question: Up to a certain time the sphere of golden light has worked very well, but I found it hard to imagine my whole self and my friend's whole self as two spheres 'facing' each other. Do you have any suggestions? I feel I should visualise a great religious

teacher like Buddha. Can you explain more?
Rinpoche: When we talk about Buddha we generally think of the historical Buddha who was born and lived in India – just as most Christians associate the qualities of Christ with the historical Jesus. But in the context of the awakened state, I am referring to whoever has that particular quality rather than to the historical Buddha specifically. So it doesn't really matter whether you regard the quality of total Enlightenment as a sphere of golden light, or Buddha-like or Christ-like; whoever, or whatever embodies that quality, only the name is different.

Question: What can I do about the part of me that keeps insisting that I'm not compassionate, not very aware, that this is all like a game of make-believe?
Rinpoche: I think if you don't have compassion the purpose of the practice is to develop it. If it were already developed, then you wouldn't need to practise in the first place.

Question: When the world is so full of cruel and violent people, how can we believe that they are all essentially compassionate and understanding? Isn't that just wishful thinking?
Rinpoche: I think that first we have to develop the right motivation. Once this has been achieved it will be possible, by means of mind-training, to see the essential purity of everyone. After that you may find the answer to your question and be able to deal with the rest.

10. Expanding and Contracting

The aim of the next exercise is to see how the solid body obstructs the flow of the mind. We all have our own sense of territory due to the existence of the physical body. We may have noticed that an unhappy mind is often associated with pain in the body, while a happy mind usually goes together with a relaxed, happy body. We all have conscious and unconscious notions about our bodies which may become very solid, inhibiting positive change and the experience of freedom. This solidity needs to be broken down. We have to get out of the grip of fixed ideas about the mind and body. The expanding and contracting exercise should help us to accomplish this.

We need to mature our minds by working with what comes up in daily situations. This can be seen as mind therapy – we are releasing ourselves from the prison of a narrow mind by allowing it to open and broaden. Thus the practice is progressive, developing in stages.

Go carefully with this meditation because it may give rise to fear. If tension or fear arise, stop meditating, relax and do one of the relaxation exercises at the beginning of the series. Do not resume the practice until you feel fully confident and relaxed. If necessary, leave it for a couple of days. If fear arises in relation to a specific part of the body, relax and allow that part of the body to become transparent in your mind's eye. Then ask, where is the fear? Who is afraid? Reflect upon this.

The Exercise

1. Expanding

Take at least five minutes 'establishing the situation'. Find yourself a comfortable sitting position with your spine upright. Feel the space around you, where you are and become aware of the sensations of the body as it is resting on the ground. Be aware of the breath as it comes in and out of the body – do relaxation breathing exercises if necessary and then start the exercise.

Begin by being aware of the sphere of golden light, embodying the qualities of wisdom and compassion, at the centre of your body. This way you avoid fear. You are the sphere of golden light so you cannot lose anything, no matter what happens to the body. Focus on every third or fourth out-breath. Expand the whole outer skin of the body outward on the outbreath so that the body keeps its shape, but assumes greater proportions. If there is any pain or discomfort in the body, focus on that area or point and let the expansion begin from there. Think of the pain flowing out with the breath as the outer skin becomes thinner and thinner. Go on expanding until you become the size of a house. Always remind yourself of your qualities as compassion and pure awareness. When you reach this size, allow the shape of the body to dissolve and continue increasing as an amorphous form.

Continue to expand, seeing the outer skin and all of the contents becoming less and less dense, until you reach the size of a mountain. At this point the body hardly exists – there is simply a fine misty outline. Continue to expand into the sky until there is no body left at all, as it has melted away into space.

If at any stage fear arises, remind yourself of your qualities of wisdom and compassion and that you cannot suffer any harm. Finally allow the complete flow of being without a body, letting go of all sense of self as well.

This phase of the exercise occupies half the session.

2. Contracting

This is the opposite of the previous exercise. Having reminded yourself that you are the sphere of golden light, the essence of wisdom and compassion, focus on the in-breath. With every third or fourth inhalation, think of the body as shrinking and dissolving into the golden light-form at your centre. Do not worry about keeping any particular shape, just continue until it dissolves completely into the sphere of golden light so that there is no 'you' left, only the expression of your pure qualities. Continue to focus on the in-breath while the sphere of golden light becomes smaller and smaller, finally shrinking to the size of a grain. Lastly the grain becomes colourless as well as transparent until it disappears completely.

This phase of the exercise occupies the second half of the session. At the end of the exercise, allow your mind to move freely wherever it wants to go. When you find yourself becoming involved with your thoughts come back to the feeling of your original body and for a few minutes practise awareness of the feeling of the breath moving in your body.

Do this exercise once a day for one hour. Continue for three weeks.

Question: As you expand outwards and upwards, should you feel yourself still in contact with your seat or the floor?
Rinpoche: It isn't at all necessary to feel stuck to your seat or the floor. The whole idea is to overcome any fear you may have of becoming one with everybody else. If, however, you feel uncomfortable about letting go completely, then you may keep some sense of contact with the ground, but sometimes it's necessary to feel you're a little higher than the ground itself.

Question: What if you find expanding more difficult to visualise than contracting, in the sense that it's difficult to stay with the

process, to feel that it's really happening?
Rinpoche: Yes, that could be a difficulty. If so, rather than trying to force anything, do some relaxation exercises and then try again.

Question: As one's body gets larger and larger, does the sphere of golden light in the heart get bigger too, or does it remain the same size?
Rinpoche: It's not really as though the sphere is a solid object hanging in the middle of the body, like a brass ball. Rather, the idea is of the sphere of golden light becoming transparent (and less substantial) as you become transparent (and less substantial), so the size doesn't matter too much.

Question: 'Expanding and Contracting' sometimes makes me feel a little unstable – what should I do about such feelings?
Rinpoche: This exercise does not have to make us feel unstable. Being able to have the feeling of being well grounded and to let go of the solid, fixed aspect of experience are not intrinsically contradictory. We can find stability in being in tune with the impermanent nature of all things and having less clinging to fixed ideas.

11. Enemy

This meditation continues the process of learning to deal with everyday situations. We are trying to find out why we think, say and do so many unnecessary, or even harmful things. In the last part of this process we came to see that since the qualities of loving kindness and understanding are in all beings, then size is of no importance. It becomes possible to increase and decrease the size of the body, as well as change its shape. Thus we begin to realise how we might free ourselves from its limitations.

In the Friend exercise we aimed to go deeper in our understanding of the other through exchanging with someone we love or like very much. The object of the present exercise is to confront aversion. Even if you don't have an enemy whom you intensely dislike, it is still possible to do this exercise because there are different categories of enemy and different degrees of enmity:

   a) Enmity based on one's own aversion: this can range in intensity from the slight, where someone frequently annoys or irritates you, to the extreme, where there is a great feeling of anger and hatred which could even make you want to kill.

   b) Enmity based on another's aversion: which is where another person sees all you do in negative terms.

   c) Enmity based on clinging: which describes a situation where you become very intensely attached to another person. In this instance, the mind always goes to that person and one is constantly preoccupied with her or him. This form of attachment might have the appearance, or label, of 'love', but it actually enslaves the mind and results in suffering.

The Exercise

Take at least five minutes 'establishing the situation'. Find yourself a comfortable sitting position with your spine upright. Feel the space around you, where you are and become aware of the sensations of the body as it is resting on the ground. Be aware of the breath as it comes in and out of the body – do relaxation breathing exercises if necessary and then start the exercise.

In this particular meditation exercise we will focus on the form and feelings of the enemy rather than the speech or activity. Begin the session by selecting a particular person who falls into one of the above categories of enmity, no matter how strong or weak the enmity may be.

Imagine that person sitting in front of you. With most of your in-breaths (not all), bring the enemy into you. Take in all of his or her feelings, sensations, thoughts, fears, inner organs and so on. With most of your out-breaths, let all of your feelings, etc. flow out of you into the enemy. This process continues until your 'qualities and attributes' and those of your enemy are fully exchanged, leaving the outer forms unchanged.

After the exchanging is complete, begin to reflect: where is the anger? Where's the hatred, the fear, the imprisoning attachment? Where is the cause of enmity? Think to yourself: 'Now that I am the enemy and the enemy is me, where is the source of the feeling?'

Having completed the exchanging and reflection, bring your own feelings back into your own form, but keep the understanding of the other. Move on to the relaxing meditation – simply allowing thoughts and feelings to flow freely. Let the mind relax and observe whatever comes and goes.

This exercise goes to the heart of our problems. It may at times be very painful, but be courageous and carry on.

Do this exercise once a day for about an hour and twenty minutes, leaving ten minutes at the end for relaxation. It is best to keep the focus on a few people, not changing too often. Continue the meditation for four weeks.

Question: If I'm having trouble with the exercise or it is giving rise to unbearable feelings of hatred and self hatred would it be useful to return to the mirror exercise?

Rinpoche: Maybe not so useful, no. In this case one could do the universal compassion exercise at the end of the book for a few days or a week, remembering to have compassion for everyone, including oneself.

Question: Although I understand that this exercise is designed to change my own mind rather than the mind of anyone else, I can't help thinking that, since I'm working so hard on myself, there ought to be some improvement in the other. Is this the wrong way to look at it?

Rinpoche: Fundamentally the idea is not to bring about change in anyone else. Whilst there may be some improvement in others, the aim and the result should be positive change in oneself.

Question: You suggest that the state of being in love could be considered as a kind of enmity. Does this mean we should run away when we feel strongly attracted to another person, or is it possible to purify the love at the heart of the attraction so that it becomes useful?

Rinpoche: If you love without clinging, or if you can overcome any clinging which may initially arise, then that love will be very, very useful. However, whenever there is clinging to the object of love, or to the idea of love itself, then the love is tainted and easily spoiled. Since clinging leads to other negative tendencies, such as expectation, possessiveness and jealousy, wherever there is clinging the purity of love is lost.

Question: While doing this exercise I've experienced the feeling of being taken over by someone whom I suspect of really wishing to harm me. This was so frightening that it was several days before I felt safe in myself again. Should I persist with the exercise in spite of this?

Rinpoche: If you're practising this exercise in a completely pure and loving way, then the idea of someone taking over your life can be seen as a very welcome development rather than as something negative. But if you're only a beginner, unable to see it in this way, it would be helpful to try and improve your understanding of the essence of compassion and wisdom within. So, should this fear arise again, try to develop awareness of the true essential nature of loving kindness and understanding within yourself, and repeat the exercise.

Question: Sometimes this exercise has a very disturbing effect on me – I get very upset and carried away by strong and bitter emotions. Is it better to carry on and try to go right through these experiences, or should I stop and practise relaxation?
Rinpoche: Both approaches have their place. At the beginning, some relaxation may be helpful; but at some stage it will be necessary to face the situation, however difficult, and overcome it. In the end it's necessary to go right through and beyond it.

Question:So far I've had no great difficulty with the exercises but coming to this one makes me feel like giving up altogether. What is the best way to deal with this?
Rinpoche: This means that the exercise is working! The whole idea is to learn how to face the situation, to overcome the difficulty of wanting to avoid obstacles. This is the benefit of the exercise. So you must go through these feelings of wanting to quit.

'Back to Beginnings' (see p. 192) is also useful as a means of clarifying and unravelling what is too difficult to face i.e. patterns of guilt and blame can be sorted out by that technique.

12.–14. Taking Suffering

General Comment

The next three exercises: Taking Suffering from Parents and Relatives, Taking Suffering from Country, Friends and Animals and Taking Suffering from Enemies go progressively deeper and deeper into our wish to benefit others. They engage our willingness to face and purify our own negative emotions in order to liberate our compassion for all beings. Once that compassion is awakened, we must put it into action by taking on the suffering of others. We cannot do this in our ordinary human form, we need the perfectly pure rainbow body of our true potential nature with all the qualities of perfect awakeness and universal compassion. The confidence developed in the previous exercises that 'I am this awakened potential' is very necessary for the meditations which follow. With the right understanding, practise visualising oneself as the 'sphere of golden light', with the deep inner conviction and confidence that this form truly represents perfect awakeness and universal compassion. If you have been visualising yourself as a Buddha or great religious teacher, then that is fine. Either way, there must be the complete confidence in your true pure nature. If that confidence is not there at present, skip to the section The Rainbow Sphere (Exercise 15 on p. 168).

12. Taking Suffering from Parents and Relatives

Up to now we have been learning to exchange ourselves with others and to see ourselves and others in rainbow form. We have seen how the mind is purely wisdom and compassion. All feelings, fears, experiences of body, speech and mind have become awakened understanding and loving kindness. Once we recognise this, it is natural we should work to help all beings. We do this by learning to take their suffering from them. We begin by taking suffering from those who are closest to us.

The Exercise

Take at least five minutes 'establishing the situation'. Find yourself a comfortable sitting position with your spine upright. Feel the space around you, where you are and become aware of the sensations of the body as it is resting on the ground. Be aware of the breath as it comes in and out of the body – do relaxation breathing exercises if necessary and then start the exercise.

Remind yourself: my true nature is perfect awareness and universal compassion, the white light of compassion is in my heart. Visualise mother, father (whether dead or alive) and close relatives in front of you. Think about each one in turn, and allow your mind to see their suffering. For example, your mother may suffer (or have suffered) from great attachment, your father may be driven by ambition, and your brother may have a physical disability. Allow all the forms of suffering which afflict your relatives to come to mind, one by one. Then choose one as the focus of your session. Breathe in. As you do so, take in all of his or her suffering, be it physical, mental, emotional or whatever. The suffering comes out in the form of a thick, black, tar-like liquid which is heavy, almost solid and unhealthy looking. With every few breaths this liquid enters your 'heart of wisdom and compassion' where the white light of compassion burns it up like fuel, creating more compassion and strengthening your awareness of your true nature.

While this is going on, with every few breaths you breathe out all goodness, virtue and happiness from your heart to him or her. The pure qualities take the form of crystal-clear white light which frees your relative from suffering and the causes of suffering. So it is a two-way process. You take suffering in the form of the black liquid, and exchange this for the pure white light.

Every now and again re-visualise the person and allow their particular sufferings to come freshly to mind. Recreate the process as often as is necessary.

As you continue with the exercise, the black liquid becomes gradually thinner and paler as the suffering is slowly removed. Finally, after about half an hour, what you breathe in is the same white light of purity as that which you breathe out. You do not need to think of this process as happening with every breath; each third or fourth breath is sufficient. Your relative has now been relieved of suffering and has become perfect wisdom and compassion, the same as you.

There is no need to fear that you will become sick or overwhelmed, because you are not your ordinary self when doing this exercise – you are visualising yourself in a light form and thus cannot suffer any harm.

Do this meditation once a day for one hour and fifteen minutes. Continue for two weeks (or longer if you wish to focus on many people), focussing on each member of your family for a few days.

13. Taking Suffering from Country, Friends and Animals

Working with feelings as we have been doing in the previous exercises helps us to free ourselves from the extremes of negative and positive emotions. First we have to overcome negative emotions and allow the arising of positive ones. The process is a gradual one and proceeds in stages.

If we develop skill and knowledge, then we have to use it. Once we have established that we are awakened wisdom and compassion, we must begin to help all beings. As beings like that we can then take on all suffering.

In our pure form, we cannot become sick. We absorb the negativities of others so that their energy, as well as our own, may be converted into compassion and loving kindness. This process of transmutation of energy continues until we reach the stage of limitless compassion.

The Exercise

The focus of this meditation will be on our country, friends

and animals. Suffering is not only that which is obvious and manifest before us. All beings are experiencing suffering – physical,
mental and emotional, in different forms. We have to learn to take
all forms of suffering from all beings. For example, by taking in
the suffering which causes attachment, i.e. desire, we remove
those factors which deny beings their freedom.

Choose a focus for your meditation: a group you are associated with or your country, an individual friend, or an animal or
group of animals. Visualise this person or persons, animal or animals in front of you.

As you breathe in, take in all forms of suffering (visualised as
in the previous exercise). As you breathe out, send the white light
of compassion that not only relieves immediate suffering but car-
ries to them whatever is most desired.

In each case, breathe out as much as you can possibly imagine
of whatever fulfils the desires which are causing the suffering so
that these desires are satisfied. Feel that the individual or the members of the group you have chosen are liberated from all attachment by getting enough of what they want. This positive white
light automatically manifests as whatever beings need in the physical, mental or emotional sense. If you know of specific needs or
attachments in people, breathe out those things in a very beautiful
form. For example, if someone badly wants a house, imagine the
most beautiful house possible – perhaps made of precious stones
and jewels – and breathe that out.

When you have completed the exercise and have fully satisfied the desires of all those beings and thus liberated them from
attachment, you see them all as pure.

Throughout the day remember: 'My true nature is utterly pure
wisdom and compassion.' Let this realisation govern all actions of
body, speech and mind. Also maintain the attitude of wanting to
help others all day. At all times, see the white light radiating out
and helping others, giving them all they desire. At the same time,
take their suffering from them. As a pure being, in a light form,
you can safely and effectively do this. Thus you develop the attitude of exchanging at all times.

It is natural sometimes to feel unequal to the task of taking all
suffering and giving out pure love and compassion. In such
moments it is important to remember that the purity of our aim is,

in the long run, our most powerful means of developing. There may appear to be a contradiction between our ideal of limitless compassion and our actual thoughts, speech and action. In fact, however, there is no contradiction because the essence of loving kindness and understanding always remains pure within us, whatever we may be going through.

Do this meditation once a day for one hour and fifteen minutes, spending two or three days on each point of focus. Continue for two weeks.

14. Taking Suffering from Enemies

We will deal with three levels of enemies in this meditation:

a) National enemies: at this level we are dealing with generalised negative forces or suffering including members of nations at war with our own, as well as with impersonal forces such as disease and drought. Emotionally, this is not such a deep level.

b) One's own enemies: those who are disliked for personal reasons, but who are not too close. There is greater depth of feeling than in a) but still not too much pain.

c) Enemies resulting from a close relationship: those friends or relatives towards whom you feel deep hatred or who feel intense hatred towards you. If you do not have such enemies, then think of an animal you particularly detest being close to.

In all these cases we will be dealing with negative emotions such as desire, jealousy and hatred. As before, the negativity comes out like a heavy tar-black liquid.

The Exercise

1. Purification:

Before attempting the taking of intense suffering from one's enemies, first one must deal with one's own mental poisons. First visualise a sphere of golden light in front of you. Focussing on the negative feelings which arise in relation to a particular enemy, allow these feelings to take form as the thick tar-black liquid mentioned above. Keeping the awareness of these impurities in yourself, open up to the purity of the golden sphere before you and allow rays of golden light to enter your body as you breathe in. As you breathe out, the negative emotions etc. will leave your body in the form of dark, black tar-like liquid.

When this leaves your body it dissolves without trace into the ground about one metre in front of you. Gradually you feel yourself filled with the golden light of the sphere; while the tar-like liquid, and the emotions it represents, becomes less dense and less solid. Now you have the conviction that you are the same as the pure light form of wisdom and compassion and are ready to take on the mental suffering of your enemies.

2. Taking a Cloud of Suffering

You imagine all of the negative forces coming from enemies to the nation, as well as those coming from acquaintances, friends and relatives. You absorb all of these at once as they enter you in the form of the black, tar-like liquid. Because your body, speech and mind is pure compassion and understanding, the negativity is burned up within you and converted into the pure white light of compassion. As the meditation proceeds, your desire to benefit and help all beings grows. When friends and others around you project the poisons, you don't attempt to escape. Instead you take them into you and give them back in the form of compassion and loving kindness.

3. Taking Suffering from an Individual Enemy

Think of someone you find difficult, and in relation to whom there is a strong negative energy in the form of hatred, jealousy or whatever. Focus on this person or animal and identify the predominant form of their suffering. Once the specific form is clear – suppose it is anger – let their anger be seen as a tar black liquid. Breathe their suffering of this into yourself. Once inside, it is burned up by the fire of compassion and is returned as the pure white light of loving-kindness. Loving-kindness can also be sent in other colours if you wish, but it mostly should be white. As in the previous exercises, the suffering becomes thinner and thinner, less and less substantial. Eventually the colour that you breathe in is of the same pure colour as that which you breathe out. The black liquid then dissolves and there is simply an exchange of clear light. Finally, you are both light forms of wisdom and compassion, and can thus understand and respect one another.

Afterwards, let your mind rest in open space for as long as it feels natural.

Do this meditation once a day for one hour and thirty minutes. Afterwards, let your mind rest in open space for as long as it feels natural. Continue for four weeks.

Question: Is it alright to do longer times for the exercises if one feels it to be useful?
Rinpoche: Yes, that is OK. The proportions of time within the exercise however should remain the same.

Question: What does the term, 'heart of wisdom and compassion' represent?
Rinpoche: It means that in the heart of your being wisdom and compassion are within you, both as potential and actuality. At this level you 'create' it but in essence it is true. You can have full confidence in this.

Question: I am quite new to this kind of exercise and I find the idea

*of taking other peoples' suffering a little frightening. Might I not
become sick?*
Rinpoche: You must remember the basic purity of your own
nature. You will not get ill by taking their suffering. The suffering
or negative emotion that you are taking in meets the white light in
the centre of the body and is thereby burned and purified. It is like
an incinerator, there is a process of purification involved. It will
help motivate us if we remember the good outcome of this exercise. Also as we are working with the mind, it is useful to remember that we should not take things in too solid a manner nor let our
imaginations run away with us. These are controlled visualisations and if we follow them correctly, there will be no harm.

*Question: Throughout this exercise much mention is made of
developing compassion but don't we need wisdom in order to do
this? Can we just rely on compassion and expect the wisdom to
come automatically?*
Rinpoche: You do need to have wisdom and compassion
together. If you are to develop a really pure compassion then there
must be wisdom. A lot will depend on how you categorise 'compassion'. If you see someone crying and you simply start crying
too, that does not solve anything. There is not much wisdom there
but if you have the understanding how to overcome their suffering and you have the technique, then the outcome will be positive.
You may both cry together but the positive outcome depends on
someone having the wisdom to help both come out of the suffering.
So you can say that you are not just looking for compassion but
wisdom as well.

In terms of relying on compassion we have to use our common sense and do the best we can now to help others if we can.
One way to wisdom is to see things as being less solid, less of a
'big deal'.

15. The Rainbow Sphere

These coloured light exercises are given to help us deal with the negative emotions that arise in our day-to-day lives. Many people experience difficulties because they fall under the power of negative emotions. Yet if we can identify these emotions, and gain insight into them, it will give us a means to understand and overcome them.

'Understanding' is a key word with regard to these exercises. For example, if we are under the influence of jealousy, we should realise how it does harm both to ourselves and others, that it restricts our freedom, and does no good to anyone. This insight will then help us want to give it up. Knowing what we are doing wrong and acknowledging its negative influence on others will motivate us to root out the causes of our negative emotions.

Some might say, 'I don't need to do such exercises because I don't have those feelings,' yet this is self-deception, arising from a failure to look in a detailed and precise way at who we are. We all have pride, anger, desire and jealousy. In all of these exercises, the first step is to recognise the negative emotion and then go on to deal with it.

The exercises use the visualisation of coloured light. Throughout all of them we should see the coloured lights as being transparent, not solid, and having a quality that is able to heal. Each colour has the essential power of all the other colours and has the ability to reduce physical pain and illness as well as emotional negativity. For example, when we have sore eyes or a headache, we can imagine the light coming into the pain, acting like medicine.

It is important that we have confidence in the coloured lights, understanding that they are the essence of medicine and do have the capacity to cure. Trust and confidence will grow as this understanding increases. With practice the colours will become easy to relate to and help us feel relaxed. The lights can be seen as the manifestations of the healing potential of our own minds. The use of visualisations to help deal with cancer is just one illustration of this potential.

There is no cure-all; sickness is a part of life and depends on many things. However, the colour meditations, even if they do not cure all our illnesses, will help us face them more easily. With faith and a very strong mind, the healing effects and benefits of the visualisations will be very strong, either immediately or later on; but if there is no faith in them, or if the mind is weak, then much less will be achieved. However, there will be no harm in doing any of the exercises.

Generally the light is to be seen as entering the body with the in-breath, and all the negative emotions and pain as being expelled with the out-breath. The light always works through the body, speech and mind, since all difficulties are related to them, and it should go wherever needed. However, it can go to the mind first since that is the source of all our actions and speech.

When doing the exercise it is as well to remember that each negative emotion is not rigidly separate from the others. For example, there can be jealous pride, stupid pride, angry pride and so on. Each colour can likewise have the benefit of all the others, even though we are focusing only on one colour at a time.

Once we have gone right through the course, we may afterwards return to these exercises to choose the one that is good for us at the time. For example, if we are unable to control our emotions due to jealousy, we may use the green light exercise as a remedy.

The Exercise

Take at least five minutes 'establishing the situation'. Find yourself a comfortable sitting position with your spine upright. Feel the space around you, where you are and become aware of the sensations of the body as it is resting on the ground. Be aware of the breath as it comes in and out of the body – do relaxation breathing exercises if necessary and then start the exercise.

First we look at the defilement, such as jealousy or pride, that has to be worked on. Recognise its harmful and disturbing consequences.

Then we imagine in front of us either a clear blue daytime sky or a night sky completely filled with stars. Whatever is most comfortable and easy to relate to.

From the distance appears a sphere of coloured lights made up of the six colours, white, green, yellow, sky-blue, red and deep blue, all jewel-like in appearance. These colours constantly move and swirl within the sphere and are brilliant and transparent like a rainbow. All of these colours then turn into one predominant colour. Feel confidence that each of these colours really has the power to remedy pain and negative emotions.

During the exercise, the light enters the body with the in-breath and helps us to deal with the negative emotions, which then leave the body in the form of unhealthy-coloured smoke and dissolve one foot away from the body. Feel that the dark-coloured smoke is being expelled with the out-breath.

There is nothing so strange about this meditation – really it is like caring for a garden – we remove the weeds and look after all that we want to cultivate.

Throughout the exercise we use our imagination and remember that each one of these healing colours has the essence of them all. If at the end of the exercise we are able ourselves to feel the benefit, then we let the healing light go out to particular individuals in need. For example, if we see someone as being very proud and we wish to help them, we can feel the light going out to her or him. After that, radiate the light out to benefit everyone.

This practice helps us to deal with our own negative emotions but it is good to remember how just doing this will help others. If, for example, we are jealous or angry, then our mood will be harmful to others because we act and move in an angry and jealous way. So the understanding and purification of the emotions in ourselves will benefit others automatically. If any tension arises, do the breathing, openness, or feeling exercises given earlier before returning to this practice.

Do each of these exercises for an hour a day for one week.

1. Visualisation of the White Light Overcoming Pride

Look at the pride within your mind. This is pride in the sense of arrogance, haughtiness and feelings of superiority over others. See its manifestations in your day-to-day life and all its effects both physical and emotional.

Visualise the rainbow-coloured sphere in front of you in the sky. All the colours swirling around in the sphere then turn into a diamond-like light, white, sparkling and pure. As you breathe in, imagine this white light coming into you, contacting and transforming the negative emotion of pride (in the sense of arrogance and feelings of superiority).

The white light streams in, making it possible to identify, understand, accept and let go of the negative kind of pride, which is then transformed into a thick black smoke that completely dissolves one foot away from the body. In the process, the light melts and washes away all of the harmful consequences of body, speech and mind caused by pride. Feel generally that the dark black smoke is being expelled with the out-breath. If you have any pain or sickness, let the diamond-like light go to that area and feel it helping you.

At the end of the session, when you are able to feel that the pride is washed away, let the light go out first to those you know and then to all others. Then visualise the white light returning to the sphere. The sphere again becomes composed of the six colours and moves away from you in space until it completely vanishes. Let your mind rest in open space for as long as feels natural.

2. Visualisation of the Green Light Overcoming Jealousy

Look at the jealousy within your mind. See its manifestations in your day-to-day life and all its effects, both physical and emotional.

Visualise the rainbow-coloured sphere in front of you in the sky. All the swirling colours merge into a rich shade of emerald green. As you breathe in, imagine this green light streaming into you, contacting and tranforming all the jealousy you experience in your body, speech and mind. This green light streams in, making it possible to identify, understand, accept and let go of the jealousy, which is then transformed into a dark green smoke that completely dissolves one foot away from the body. If you have any pain or sickness, let the incoming green light go to that area and feel it helping you.

At the end of the session, when you feel that the jealousy is washed away, let the light go out first to people you know and then to everyone. Visualise the green light returning to the sphere. The sphere again becomes composed of the six colours and moves away from you in space until it completely vanishes. Afterwards, let your mind rest in open space for as long as feels natural.

3. Visualisation of the Yellow Light Overcoming Desire and Frustration

Look at the feelings of desire and frustration in your life. Notice any sensations in the body associated with these emotions.

Visualise the rainbow-coloured sphere in front of you in the sky. All the swirling colours merge into a rich, bright, golden yellow. As you breathe in, imagine the yellow light coming into you, contacting and transforming all the feelings of unfulfilled desire, dissatisfaction, discontent and frustration you experience in your body, speech and mind. The yellow light streaming in makes it possible to identify, understand, accept and let go of these negative feelings, which are then transformed into a dark yellow smoke that completely dissolves one foot away from the body. If you have any pain or sickness, let the yellow light go to that area and feel it helping you.

At the end of the session, after feeling that the desire and frustration is washed away, let the light go out first to those you know and then to all others. Then visualise the yellow light returning to the sphere. The sphere again becomes composed of the six colours and moves away from you in space until it completely vanishes. Then let your mind rest in open space for as long as feels natural.

4. Visualising the Sky-Blue Light Overcoming Stupidity

Look within your mind and see where there is complacency, dullness and stupidity. See its manifestations in your day-to-day life and all its effects, both physical and emotional. As before, imagine the sphere appearing in front of you in the wide open space.

All the colours swirling around in the sphere then merge into a clear sky-blue. As you breathe in, imagine the blue light coming into you from the sphere, contacting and transforming all the dullness and stupidity of body, speech and mind. This blue light streaming in makes it possible to identify, understand, accept and let go of these feelings, which are then transformed into a dark-blue smoke that dissolves one foot away from the body. If you have any pain or sickness let the light go to that area and feel it helping you.

At the end of the session, after feeling that the dullness and stupidity is washed away, let the light go out first to those you know and then to all others. Then visualise the blue light returning to the sphere. The sphere again becomes composed of the six colours and moves away from you in space until it completely vanishes. Then let your mind rest in open space for as long as feels natural.

5. Visualising the Ruby-Red Light Overcoming Craving

Look within your mind, not only at insatiable craving but also at the feelings of poverty, loneliness, meanness and the inability to share with others. See their manifestation in your day-to-day life and all their effects, both physical and emotional.

Visualise the rainbow-coloured sphere in front of you in the sky. All the colours merge into a cheerful, ruby red. The colour has a feeling of richness and friendliness about it. As you breathe in, imagine the red light coming into you, contacting and transforming the kind of feelings described earlier. This red light streaming in makes it possible to identify, understand, accept and let go of these feelings, which are then transformed into a dark-brown smoke that dissolves one foot away from the body. In the process, the light melts and dissolves away all of the harmful consequences of body, speech and mind caused by craving and meanness etc. For example, see how your craving disturbs others and distresses you – then visualise the red light remedying this craving. If you have any pain or sickness, let the cheerful red light go to that area and feel it helping you.

At the end of the session (after feeling that all is purified) let the light go out first to those you know and then to all others. Then visualise the red light returning to the sphere. The sphere again becomes composed of the six colours and moves away from you in space until it completely vanishes. Let your mind rest in open space for as long as feels natural.

6. Visualising the Blue-Black Light Overcoming Anger

Look at the feelings of anger and hatred in your mind. See their harmful consequences in your day-to-day life, both physical and emotional.

As before, visualise the rainbow-coloured sphere appearing in front of you in the sky. All the colours merge into a blue-black colour that has a jewel-like sparkling quality. As you breathe in, imagine this deep-blue light coming into you, contacting and transforming all the anger and hatred in your body, speech and mind. This deep-blue light makes it possible to identify, understand, accept and let go of the anger and hatred which is then transformed into a dirty, black smoke that dissolves one foot away from the body. Let the deep-blue sparkling light go to any areas of pain or sickness that you have and feel it benefitting you.

At the end of the session when all the anger and hatred is washed away, let the light go out first to those you know and then to all others. Then visualise the deep-blue light returning to the sphere, which again becomes composed of the six colours and moves away from you in space until it completely vanishes. Afterwards, let your mind rest in open space for as long as feels natural.

Question: Sometimes I feel like I'm getting stuck – the same kind of images or things are recurring all the time, even when I am doing different meditations or visualisations. What is the advice for this kind of problem?
Rinpoche: I think it is good to rest the mind a little.

Question: But I feel I'm getting very angry because I'm making no progress, and I feel quite negative about the exercise.
Rinpoche: If you have anger and think there is no progress, I think that is progress because before you were unaware of being angry. If you realise there is anger, this is also a means for making progress. It's like cleaning a table – if it hasn't been cleaned for years, then you don't see each individual speck of dust – it's just one thick cloud. If you clean a table once a month, then you can

see the new dust. If you clean it every day, then you can see each bit of dust. Still there is dust, but it can be seen very clearly.

16. Universal Compassion

We must understand the need to put these exercises into use in a total way – fully engaging our body, speech and mind in them. In order to allow the mind to mature, we have to dig negativities out at the root. If we do these exercises thoroughly we will have no need to look outside for therapy.

The Exercise

Take at least five minutes 'establishing the situation'. Find yourself a comfortable sitting position with your spine upright. Feel the space around you, where you are and become aware of the sensations of the body as it is resting on the ground. Be aware of the breath as it comes in and out of the body – do relaxation breathing exercises if necessary and then start the exercise.

This exercise connects breathing with the Four Limitless Meditations (below), and enables us to generate full loving-kindness. For the first half of the session imagine the suffering, unhappiness, and lack of peace of all beings (coming into you generally with the in-breath). In the second half of the session, synchronised with the out-breath, think:

'May all beings always have happiness and the causes of happiness. May they all be free from suffering and the causes of suffering. May each one never be separate from the true happiness which is beyond suffering. May they always act with understanding of the great impartiality, free from attachment to close ones and aversion to others.'

Remain for one quarter of the second session on each of the four lines of the prayer.

Do this exercise for half an hour a day for four weeks. Throughout the day in the post-meditation period, think of these Four Limitless Meditations as much as you can. Try to develop a good understanding of them.

All these meditation exercises are part of the slow process of changing the mind to prepare for the development of positive qualities. Negativities cannot be expected to vanish at once, but gradually the ground is prepared, and then changes take place, little by little.

17. The Universe Transformed by Compassion

Preliminary Explanation

This exercise deals with the three areas of body, speech and mind as we experience them ordinarily and as they may be experienced when transformed by Universal Compassion. These three areas can cover all our experience from the time we are born until we die.

In Tibetan tradition, the body aspect is related to through the head, specifically through a point in the centre of the forehead. This is especially useful for many Westerners since we tend not to recognize the head enough as part of the body. Relating to the body through the head helps us to remember their unity.

The speech aspect is related to through a point at the base of the throat.

The mind aspect is reached through a point at the level of the heart in the centre of the body.

In each case, we use a colour of light to transmit the healing power of Universal Compassion.

At some time in their lives most people experience healing whether it be through antibiotics, a healer, a friend, an inner experience, or something in the outer environment. All healing can be seen as a manifestation of Universal Compassion which we can invite to help us in the three areas of body, speech and mind.

The white light of Universal Compassion especially heals the body and our relationship with the material level of reality.

The red light works to heal the speech. The speech centre at the base of the throat is related to positive feelings such as love, joy and creative expression. All of the wanting and dissatisfaction of past, present and future can also be most powerfully experienced in this centre. Likewise it can all be healed there. This applies especially to feelings of dissatisfaction related to emotional needs for love, joy and creative expression. This links up with the idea of speech – that we can speak our feelings and give of ourselves freely and openly.

The blue light of Universal Compassion especially heals the mind and acts as an antidote to fear, anxiety and mental confusion.

Instructions follow for the use of the three lights for healing body, speech and mind. However we do not have to take it too literally. If you are unable to relate to it, just stay with your own experience and maintain the key concept of the healing power of Universal Compassion. Remember this Compassion is always available if you are able to open up to it.

The deeper purpose of the exercise is to prepare you to recognize the intrinsic purity and perfection of the universe in all phenomena as they reveal themselves when compassion has purified your perception and you are free from the distortion of ego-based perception.

The Exercise

Preparation: generate within yourself a feeling of compassion.

Start every session by contemplating briefly the Four Limitless Meditations:

'May all beings have happiness and the causes of happiness May they all be free from suffering and the causes of suffering May each one never be separate from the true happiness which has no suffering, And may they always act with understanding of the great impartiality, free from attachment to close ones and aversion to others.'

If this traditional formulation causes you any problem, simply fill yourself with a feeling of compassion, wishing no-one to suffer any longer.

Healing and Transformation by the Lights of Compassion

Establishing the situation

Make yourself comfortable sitting with a straight spine, but with no strain. If you cannot relax sitting, you can lie down, but it may be more difficult to feel the three centres one above another.

Begin by relaxing, feeling the breath moving in and out of the body. Feel that each time you breathe out you are able to let go of some disturbance, irritation, solidness or discomfort. Each out-breath is a letting go – clearing the way for the work you are going to do. Allow your mind to wander freely through the body, feeling sensations everywhere. Simply recognize whatever is there – tension, pain or discomfort. Keep your attention moving, not stopping too long in any one area.

Imagine before you a completely open sky. Try to relate to the unobstructed quality of the space in all directions.

Three horizontal bands of light appear, equal in width: dazzling white on top, warm ruby red in the centre, and deep cornflower blue at the bottom. These may be seen as vast, stretching from horizon to horizon and filling your whole field of vision, or as just covering one area of space in front of you.

Imagine that you have before you an active manifestation of Universal Compassion expressed through these three colours. Without using any special effort to see these colours, feel that they are really there – very light and very bright, very pure and insubstantial like rainbow light.

First of all, focus on the white band of light. This very brilliant, sparkling, diamond-clear white light enters the body through a point at the centre of the forehead and then circulates very freely throughout the body, bringing the healing of Universal Compassion. If it is difficult to imagine the light entering through the one point, feel it comes in with the breath, or, as your body is non-solid, it may enter everywhere like rain. Whichever way you see it, feel that all pain, sickness and tension are dissolved as the iridescent white light circulates ever more freely until you feel your whole body is purified and transparent.

Now return to your own experience. Feel yourself in your body and become aware of your feelings in the sense of emotions. Open up to feelings of frustration, dissatisfaction, suppression of creativity and joy. Be aware of any past or present feelings of being deprived of love, beauty, education, companionship, intelligence. Allow any feelings of discontent, resentment and alienation to arise. Likewise be aware of the envy and jealousy that such feelings arouse, also the panic and confusion of not getting what you feel you need and desire.

Consider also whatever you wish to give to others or express of yourself where you feel the expression is blocked or never has a chance to come to life.

Now again, become aware of the three bands of light, the colours of Universal Compassion before you in the sky.

This time, focus on the ruby red band of light.

This is a very cheerful, happy colour which gives a feeling of joy, spontaneity and love. The colour is never heavy or bloody, but joyful and easy to relate to. Feel that the remedy for all your craving, dissatisfaction and frustrated expression can come to you through this pure red light of compassion. Feel that it enters your body through a point at the base of the throat, or through the breath, or everywhere like rain, but whichever way it comes, it streams freely through the body bringing a feeling of joy, love and complete fulfilment. It also dissolves all obstacles to clear speech and creative expression of all kinds. The light travels, without obstruction, bringing the pure and complete healing of Universal Compassion. This light sets you free to feel joy, love and compassion, and no matter what has happened in the past, you are free to feel and express this.

Now go back to your own experience and this time allow yourself to consider fear as you have experienced it. This can be fear ranging from the slightest level of nervousness, anxiety, self-consciousness, petty insecurity, right through to the most overwhelming fears of death, disaster and madness. Likewise consider fear of facing yourself and facing other people, along with your experiences of confusion, lack of clarity and mental instability.

Now again, we see the three bands of light, the three active manifestations of Universal Compassion before us. This time we focus on the deep, intense blue light at the bottom. This colour like cornflowers, like lapis lazuli in the form of light, gives a feeling of great courage, confidence, stability and clarity of mind. Compassion in this form heals all kinds of fear, anxiety, insecurity and confusion, bringing instead a sense of courage, calm and relaxed stability.

Feel the blue light coming towards you and entering the body at the level of the heart. This beautiful deep-blue light has a special power to heal all the fears, worries and distortions of the mind. Whether the blue light enters through the one point, or with the breath, or everywhere like the rain, whichever way it comes in, the blue light of compassion circulates freely throughout the body, bringing a feeling of courage, openness and stability, healing all suffering of the mind.

Feel now that the light of compassion has purified you totally – body, speech and mind. You are now perfectly pure in all aspects of your being, physically, verbally, emotionally and mentally.Your whole being has been transformed into compassion.

Transformation of the Whole Universe through Compassion

Imagine now that the three colours of the light of compassion, that are still there in front of you in the sky, begin to shine brilliantly and fill the whole universe with white, red and blue rays.

Think that the light illuminates this whole galaxy and others beyond our known world, and all that is part of it, is totally purified and transformed. The whole universe becomes a paradise – a world of purity, perfection and complete happiness.

All sounds heard are infinitely beautiful and pure; they are the spontaneous outcome, the natural expression of perfection.

All thoughts that animate the universe, whatever their form or manner, even the smallest movements of the mind represent the very essence of perfection.

If you are really concerned with the problems or the suffering of a country or people or some person in particular, you can think of them when the light of compassion fills the universe; imagine that it touches them specially.

The Last Stage

Stay absorbed in this state of perfection as long as it seems natural to you. Finish as you started in the preparation by contemplating for a while the four limitless thoughts, or generate the feeling of compassion.

Practice this exercise for four weeks, half an hour a day.

N.B. If you wish to emphasize one of these areas of healing, e.g. the white light for the body, you can spend longer on this but always include all three bands of light in the visualisation.

Afterword

The contents of this book have been offered as course material to various groups in approximately twenty different places in Britain, Ireland, the USA and South Africa, over a period of ten years.

It was at the request of Dr Akong Tulku Rinpoche that I began teaching courses in massage and relaxation, weaving in more and more material from 'Taming the Tiger'. I would then bring any questions or problems arising in the courses back to Akong Rinpoche. His answers would then be incorporated into later courses, as well as into the text of the book. All who have taken part in these courses have contributed to this book, as have many of my therapy clients in Edinburgh who have tried a variety of these exercises and reported back the results.

The response to the material has been positive from the beginning. There are quite a few people who have written to me long after attending a particular course, expressing the benefits of working with the exercises, both for health and self-development. Some people who have been practising meditation for ten years or more have found the 'simple-mindedness' of this approach has helped them get over spiritual ambitiousness and other blocks to genuine meditation. Others have found the advice and sequence of exercises very practical, down to earth and easy to incorporate into everyday life.

Those who are willing to go 'back to kindergarten' and consider the beginnings and simplest forms of their experience are those who will find it easiest to benefit. It will take nearly a year to complete the material in this book even for those who practise every day. However, this should not be seen as an end to therapy. Rather it could be the beginning of true therapy – working with the world just as it is and with ourselves just as we are – from now to the end of our lives.

Edith Irwin, M.A.

Biography of the Second Akong Tulku

The qualities of simplicity and directness in living and teaching the Buddhadharma characterise the life of the Second Akong Tulku. He himself sees his life in terms of three main phases. The early life he spent in Tibet; second, the life he spent in India; third, his life and teaching in the West.

The First Akong Tulku had so many qualities that, after his death in 1938, the people at Dolma Lhakang asked His Holiness the Karmapa to find his reincarnation. This had been achieved by 1942; and the 3-year-old Akong Rinpoche was enthroned. He returned to his home after this and then, at the age of 6, he entered the monastery. Then he began the intensive training and followed the teachings given to tulkus. Among his many distinguished teachers were His Holiness the Karmapa, Trungpa Rinpoche, Rolpe Rinpoche and Dingo Chentse Rinpoche. One of his root teachers was Sechen Kongtrul Rinpoche (who was also the teacher of Trungpa Rinpoche).

In his youth, he undertook a six-month retreat and also specialised in the study of medicine, both because of his own interest and also because there was a strong medical tradition at his monastery. His life-long enthusiasm for medicine and therapeutic meditation techniques has continued to develop in order to help people wherever he teaches.

In Tibet, he had the responsibility for one monastery, four nunneries and a retreat centre. He gave teachings to people in retreat and also to lay people as well as to the thousand or so monks and nuns who were at Dolma Lhakang (the name of the area over which he had authority). Akong Rinpoche has deep gratitude for the teachers who taught him the Dharma in Tibet.

At the age of 20, the Chinese invasion forced Akong Rinpoche to leave the country and he made the escape with Trungpa Rinpoche and a large group of Tibetans, lay people and monks.

The journey was very difficult and involved much hardship.

Thus, in 1959, Rinpoche arrived in India, where he was to stay for four years. The first year was especially difficult, becoming acquainted with an unfamiliar society, new customs and a different language. (He is very grateful to the late Sister Palmo (Mrs. Freda Bedi) who adopted and gave a home to both Akong Rinpoche and Trungpa Rinpoche.) In the second year there, he became responsible for looking after the home for young lamas in Delhi. In general, in India, he met many people from all ranks of society (including Mr. Nehru) and began to learn about and understand Western ideas.

In 1963, he came to the West and then lived in Oxford for four years. Whilst there, he worked in a hospital and is very grateful to Dr. Bent Juel-Jensen both for his personal kindness and also for giving him valuable insights into the way Western medicine is conducted. This was especially helpful since Akong Rinpoche's position at the hospital was low in status because his Tibetan qualifications were not recognised in the West.

At Oxford, many people were interested in Tibetan meditation techniques and culture and so it was decided to buy a property where Trungpa and Akong Rinpoches could teach, in Scotland. This was how Samyé Ling was established in 1967. In 1969 Trungpa Rinpoche left for America. Since then Akong Rinpoche has been in charge of Samyé Ling.

The Samyé Ling Tibetan Centre has grown very much from these small beginnings and now has several dozen affiliated centres all over Europe and South Africa. Rinpoche tries to give a course in each of the centres at least once a year and is tireless in carrying out the wishes of the people concerned. At Samyé Ling, visitors always have the opportunity to see him personally for guidance and instruction.

At Samyé Ling, Rinpoche has built the largest Buddhist temple in Western Europe, which accommodates several hundred people in the main shrine room. The way Samyé Ling and the other affiliated centres develop is a demonstration of Rinpoche's talent for organisation. He shows great compassion and patience towards his students, and humility is something he not only teaches but practises in his daily life. Even this book arose out of the request of his students and not out of a desire on his part for fame or gain.

In 1983, he revisited Tibet and was asked to take over responsibility for several monasteries. Akong Rinpoche is a fully accomplished master of Vajrayana and has the deep Mahamudra Transmission. He teaches on a vast range of subjects according to the needs of his students. He is well known for his understanding of the Western condition and for invaluable spiritual advice and guidance.

Appendix

Over the last twelve years, Akong Rinpoche has emphasised therapy as a valuable way of working on oneself and the situations and obstacles in daily life. He draws upon a profound knowledge of the mind from his Buddhist training and realisation, and from his expertise in Tibetan medicine, to create a way of therapy especially suitable for Westerners living ordinary lives. He has presented his approach to therapy through courses at Samyé Ling, and elsewhere in the British Isles, Europe, Africa, the United States and Canada, and thus has a broad overview of the needs of people in many parts of the world. Although his therapy teaching is diverse according to need and condition, the underlying focus is to enable people to mature and develop their own understanding and universal compassion.

One might wonder why a fully qualified meditation master would choose to work with people in a therapeutic way rather than keeping entirely to meditation. Akong Rinpoche's wish and commitment is to work for the immediate and the long-term benefit of all who might seek his help. This includes many people who have no interest in Buddhism, meditation or religion, but who recognise that they need help to enable themselves to overcome problems related to stress, confusion, anxiety and emotional immaturity.

Rinpoche has made the decision to present his therapeutic teachings in a five-year programme. For those already qualified as therapists who wish to undertake the training, the timing and requirements will be quite precise. For others who undertake the course for their own development it would be spread over a much longer period. However the sequence of topics and exercises follow one from another; the maturity gained from one becomes the basis for practising the next. Four years of the five-year training programme is already available. The sequence so far is:

Back to Beginnings

This is a preliminary investigation of our life as a whole and it helps us to see who we really are. It provides a structure for looking at negative and positive experience in a more balanced way. The method includes writing, drawing, painting and simple massage, relaxation,visualisation, work with the 'Five Elements' and regular group meetings. The work is self-motivated, but the group is important for friendship and support as well as for working on problems encountered in coordinating ourselves with others.

At the end of about eighteen months there is a week planned for re-experiencing the phase of life from conception through birth. The group then continues to meet regularly for at least two months afterwards to do further work with the Elements and to integrate birth experience with everyday life.

'Working with the Elements' (Phase one) is meant to be practised within the first year of 'Back to Beginnings'. It is based on a view of life where what makes up the individual is no different from what makes up the universe. The first phase involves exploring each of the five elements: earth, water, fire, air and space. They are investigated as they appear in nature, and how we relate to each one physically and emotionally within ourselves.

The second phase, 'Balancing the Elements Within', involves visualising the pure essence of each element as a non-solid form. This comes at the end of the 'Back to Beginnings' process and helps to stabilise emotions while integrating the birth experience into everyday experience.

Taming the Tiger

This programme covers a little more than one year. It is a series of therapy exercises given by Akong Rinpoche and published in this book. These are practised in order, both in group meetings and working individually on one's own. The group will continue to integrate massage, drawing, painting and mutual support with the practice of the exercises.

The Six Realms

The Six Realms is a six-month course investigating the origins, attributes and consequences of dwelling in the six negative emotional states:

1. Pride
2. Jealousy
3. Desire and Busyness
4. Stupidity
5. Greed and Craving
6. Anger and Hatred

   Each state and our experience of it is explored, and how each state arises within us and combines with and leads to the others. Then we investigate and explore antidotes of various sorts, mainly through practising awareness and visualisation. The group work involves movement as well as drawing and painting.

More Information

Those interested in more information may contact Samyé Ling or Tara Rokpa Trust, Edinburgh. Tara Rokpa Trust Booklets on Back to Beginnings and Working with the Elements as well as Relaxation Tapes are available at £5 each from the Tara Rokpa Trust, 45 East Trinity Road, Edinburgh EH5 3DL, Scotland.

For information about the therapy programme, contact:

Tara Rokpa Edinburgh,
45 East Trinity Road,
Edinburgh EH5 3DL,
Scotland.
Tel/fax: 031 552 1431

Jennifer Cleary,
ROKPA USA,
P.O. Box 6071,
Boulder,
CO 80306
USA.
Tel/fax (303) 447-1511

Marjorie Epp,
133 Sicamore Place,
Fort McMurray,
Alberta T9H 3RY
Canada.
Tel: (403) 743-5774

Dorothy Gunne, M.A., M. Psych. Sc., A.F.P.s S.I.,
8 Granite Terrace,
Inchicore,
Dublin 8,
Ireland.
Tel: 3531 4 542453

Carol Sagar, B.A. Hons, A.T.C, Dip. A.Th, R.A.Th.,
The Maisonette,
St Cecilia's,
13 Sea View Road,
Mundesley,
Norfolk,
NR11 8DH
UK.
Tel: 0263 721 493

Dr. Isaac Sobol, B.A., M.D., C.C.F.P.,
ROKPA CANADA
P.O. Box 229,
New Aiyansh,
British Columbia
V0J 1AO
Canada.
Tel: (604) 633-2644
Fax: (604) 633-2638

Dr Brion Sweeney, M.B., Med. Sc., M.R.C., Psych.,
4 Grattan Court,
Inchicore,
Dublin 8,
Ireland.
Tel/fax: 3531 4545923

Trish Swift, M. Soc. Sc.,
22 Harris Road,
Highlands,
Harare,
Zimbabwe.
Tel: 2634 48394

Dona Witten, B.A.,
4958 Wintersong Lane,
Westerville,
Ohio 43081
U.S.A.
Tel: (614) 794-229

❖

Power Places of Kathmandu

HINDU AND BUDDHIST HOLY SITES
IN THE SACRED VALLEY OF NEPAL
Photography by Kevin Bubriski
Text by Keith Dowman
ISBN 0-89281-540-X •10 1/2 x 13 1/2
108 color photographs • $39.95 cloth

In Nepal's Kathmandu Valley, power places—focal points of divine energy—open their windows into the Abode of the Gods. From simple landforms revered since ancient times to elaborate temples replete with stone, wood, and bronze sculpture, these sites have for centuries been revered by both Hindus and Buddhists.

During a ten-year stay in Nepal, internationally award-winning photographer Kevin Bubriski captured on film the mystery and grandeur of these sacred sites, and his evocative photographs of the people and places come to life in this handsome oversize volume. The history and significance of more than thirty of the most important sites are detailed by noted scholar and Kathmandu resident Keith Dowman.

Power Places of Kathmandu is organized according to the actual routes used by pilgrims through the three Old Kingdoms of Nepal: Kathmandu, Patan, and Bhaktapur. Through the lens of the photographer you will see a vital and vibrant spirituality practiced as it has been for centuries in this remote paradise. From quiet devotions in misty morning light to exuberant religious processions that sweep you away in a rush of color, both spiritual seekers and armchair travelers will find treasures seldom seen by Western eyes.

The Meditator's Guidebook

PATHWAYS TO GREATER AWARENESS AND CREATIVITY
Lucy Oliver
ISBN 0-89281-360-1 • $9.95 paperback

A teacher of meditation explains the basic process of meditation, describing its benefits and pitfalls, and shows how patient observation, concentration, and volition can bring calmness, power, and insight to the practitioner.

Masters of Enchantment

THE LIVES AND LEGENDS OF THE MAHASIDDHAS
Keith Dowman • Illustrated by Robert Beer
ISBN 0-89281-224-9 • $19.95 paperback
32 full-color illustrations • Line art throughout

This beautifully illustrated collection of stories, skillfully retold from the original twelfth century A.D. text, tells the legends of the saints and magicians who founded the lineages of the Tantric Buddhist tradition. Extraordinary men and women from all walks of life, the Mahasiddhas demonstrate that enlightenment may be found in the most unexpected circumstances.

"We are drawn into the Mahasiddhas' magnificent magical vision of the universe, and we can take innocent delight in their often quirky personalities, their tremendous sense of humor, and their penchant for miraculous feats. This volume is an exemplary achievement and should be in the hands of every student of spirituality." **Spectrum Review**

The Sacred Mountain of Tibet

ON PILGRIMAGE TO KAILAS
Russell Johnson and Kerry Moran
ISBN 0-89281-325-3 • $24.95 cloth
More than 100 color plates

Spectacular color photography and vivid narrative lead you through the Himalayas to Kailas, a majestic mountain held sacred by both Hindu and Buddhist for more than 1,000 years. During the few years that Westerners were permitted to visit this area of Tibet, the authors joined a group of pilgrims on the path of devotion around Kailas and were able to record a rare glimpse of a region and a ritual almost unknown in the West.

"Both the vivid description and the awe-inspiring color photographs help to capture the mystical experience of this region and its religious significance." **Booklist**

"Explores what a mountain in Tibet means to the people who live near it all their lives—a welcome change from books which acknowledge the Himalayas only as a challenge for Western mountaineers." **Vogue**

Zen and the Psychology of Transformation

The Supreme Doctrine

Hubert Benoit • Introduction by Aldous Huxley
ISBN 0-89281-272-9 • $12.95 paperback

While Western psychology tends to focus on problems rather than possibilities, Zen thought seeks to activate true human potential. In this classic work, Benoit, a psychiatrist, advocates an integration of East and West in which Western psychology is informed and enriched by Zen thought.

"The ancient Zen masters would have given Benoit their imprimatur. He has understood their secret and made it his own."   **London Times**

The Buddhist Handbook

A Complete Guide to Buddhist Schools, Teaching, Practice, and History

John Snelling
ISBN 0-89281-319-9 • $16.95 paperback

This is the first book to provide an overview of Buddhism worldwide—the different schools, concepts, interpretations, teachers, and organizations, from its early history, meditation practices, and festivals through the Westward migration of Buddhist thought. It also includes a Who's Who of Buddhism from a modern Western perspective.

Zen in Motion

Lessons from a Master Archer on Breath, Posture, and the Path of Intuition

Neil Claremon
ISBN 0-89281-361-X • $10.95 paperback

With simplicity, depth, and humor, Zen archer Neil Claremon tells the story of his own training with a Japanese master, and shows how you can adapt this process to related areas of spiritual study. From assuming a basic stance to shooting from a running horse, he describes techniques for breathing, standing, walking, concentrating, moving the mind, overcoming the ego, and healing the body, and explains the space between stillness and motion that allows the expansion of time and consciousness.

The Doctrine of Awakening

THE ATTAINMENT OF SELF-MASTERY
ACCORDING TO THE EARLY BUDDHIST TEXTS

Julius Evola

ISBN 0-89281-553-1 • $16.95 paperback

In a probing analysis of the oldest Buddhist texts, Evola places the doctrine of liberation in its original context. The early teachings suggest an active spirituality that is opposed to the more passive, modern forms of theistic religions. This sophisticated, highly readable text, first published in Italian in 1943, sets forth the central truths of the eight-fold path. Evola presents actual practices of concentration and visualization and places them in the larger metaphysical context of the Buddhist model of mind and universe.

Creative Visualization

Ronald Shone

ISBN 0-89281-214-1 • $9.95 paperback

It is widely recognized that people can create transformations in their lives by generating powerful imagery. This book explores the practical application of visualization techniques in business, sports, and personal development, showing you how to use creative visualization to realize life goals.

Centering

A GUIDE TO INNER GROWTH

Sanders Laurie and Melvin Tucker

ISBN 0-89281-420-9 • $9.95 paperback

Offering a unique system of meditation techniques, *Centering* helps you increase personal learning power and healing energy, discover new talents within yourself, and ultimately learn how to live at ease in a stressful world.

These and other Inner Traditions titles are available at many fine bookstores or, to order directly from the publisher, send a check or money order for the total amount, payable to Inner Traditions, plus $3.00 shipping and handling for the first book and $1.00 for each additional book to:

Inner Traditions, One Park Street, Rochester, VT 05767